D1366968

TAHITI

TAHITI

by Barnaby Conrad

A STUDIO BOOK   THE VIKING PRESS   NEW YORK

For Geraldine and Winston Cowgill

CONTENTS

PART 1

When a man's been given a bad time by his boss, when his wife's made him feel inadequate as a husband and father, when he's caught his mistress cheating on him, when the insurance premiums and car payments smolder unpaid and unpayable on the desk, to where does a man think of escaping?

Canada? Venice? Bombay? Tokyo? If he's like most of us, he'll stare out the window and dream a familiar juvenile dream of the South Seas, and in the minds of most men that is Tahiti-nui-mare-'are-a, Great Tahiti of the Golden Haze.

H. M. Tomlinson once observed, "there are place names which when whispered privately, have the unreasonable power of translating the spirit east of the sun and west of the moon. They cannot be seen in print without a thrill." For nearly two hundred years an island no longer than thirty miles and no wider than eighteen has captivated the romantic imagination of men as no other place in the world has ever been able to do. Men have used adjectives and similes they wouldn't dare ascribe to any other place in the universe.

Bougainville declared, "I thought I was walking in the Garden of Eden."

Captain Cook said, "Scarcely a spot in the universe affords a more luxurious prospect."

Darwin said, "Far more magnificent than anything I had ever before beheld."

R. L. Stevenson, about the Tahitians: "God's best—at least, God's sweetest."

Rupert Brooke: "There the Eternals are, and there the Good, the Lovely, and the True."

Pretty big words, pretty brave statements.

And why? What does Tahiti have, besides such good press agents as R. L. Stevenson, Pierre Loti, Frederick O'Brien, Herman Melville, Somerset Maugham, Joseph Conrad, Gauguin, and Nordhoff and Hall? Probably more books have been written about Tahiti than about any other island except England, and I had read just about every one, plus dozens of magazine articles, since I was fifteen, but I still didn't know what the place was really like till I came here a few years ago. In this book I will try to give it to you without succumbing to the overripe adjectives, the wishful thinking, and the romance of the past which so often clouds writings about Polynesia. We'll try to do it by using my own observations, honest quotations from a dozen or so writers I've admired, and true photographs.

Before we get to the woman question (which seems to be uppermost in the minds of prospective travelers, both the males and their apprehensive wives) let's list a few things that Tahiti, at this writing, does *not* have, and in so doing we will indirectly be explaining something about why this place can charm the harassed American even more than it charmed Captain Bligh's sailors back in 1788.

Tahiti has no newspaper, television, juvenile delinquency, stop lights, tipping, suicide, neon, golf course (but see page 143), murder, billboards, rape, PTA, trains, psychiatrists, or—since the houses don't have locks—locksmiths.

Of how many other places in the world is this still true? No wonder writers have to struggle to resist employing the tired phrase, "the last paradise."

The most obvious evidence of modern life on the island is the new-fangled modes of transportation; there are over one thousand cars, generally little Renaults, another couple of thousand scooters or bicycles with motors, and—horrors!—outriggers with outboards. This is the biggest difference in the Tahiti of today compared to yesteryear; otherwise, it has changed very little, probably less than any other place in the modern world. The main reason it has maintained its charm over the centuries has been its inaccessibility.

First of all, the French have always discouraged tourism there. They want no *touristes bananes,* as they refer to would-be beachcombers—types who intend to live off bananas and coconuts in a thatched hut. Before being granted a visa you must show ability to support yourself without a job and you must have a return ticket. Secondly, travel facilities have been expensive and awkward. For example, in 1959 I took the Matson Line's direct cruise from San Francisco and it cost around $1200 before I was through. I flew back, and, what with changing planes and waiting at Bora Bora, Fiji, and Honolulu, it took four exhausting days and cost another $1200.

Now the travel picture has changed virtually overnight, and Tahiti, which has so bravely resisted the advance of civilization, may be doomed. Some gloomy old-timers are saying that in ten years Papeete will be just another Waikiki. Others say that Tahiti is made of sterner stuff and will never change much. Tahiti has always been an expensive plaything for the French—albeit so beloved a one that they didn't mind

Looking at Mooréa—the original "Bali-ha'i"—from a few miles out of Papeete.

FRED LYON

putting out millions of francs a year to maintain it; but now they simply can't afford it. De Gaulle gave the order that the island must pay its own way. With the income from copra and phosphate dwindling, the French realized that there was only one way for the virginal pearl of the Pacific to make money: to submit to the lusts of tourists, mainly *les Americains* with all those nice heavy dollars in their seersucker pockets.

So Tahiti is being sacrificed to the biggest tourist boom in recent travel history, and no one is happy about it except those for whom profit is all, and they are rubbing their hands with glee. And with reason, *mon vieux*; there used to be a scant three thousand tourists, and they are now talking in terms of fifty thousand American visitors a year!

The long-time resident foreign colony of Tahiti is sick at the thought, but the Tahitians themselves couldn't care less. The French are revolted by the possibility of this lovely place being strewn with cola bottles and awash with pale, Brownie-snapping tourists, yet they shrug and ask, What is one to do? Actually, what they would like most of all—only they haven't figured out a way to say it diplomatically—is to ask us just to stay home and send our money to them in an envelope.

The blame for the rape of Tahiti rests squarely on the Wright brothers. The island had no airport before 1961; the once-a-week plane service was offered on wonderful vintage British flying boats that took off from the lagoon and connected with other islands, such as Aitutaki and Bora Bora, that did have landing strips. Now that lovely lagoon has been filled in for a jet port (see page 137), and Tahiti will never be quite the same.

So should you pack up and rush down to Tahiti quickly before it gets ruined? The answer is the one I give to people asking whether they should get married or not: if there's any doubt in your mind, don't. Tahiti depends upon who you are, what you want, and what you expect the island to be. Eugene Burdick stated in *Holiday* magazine that all

Americans have a fixed idea of what Polynesia should be and nothing can dissuade them.

I had a neat, precise and colorful vision of what it was like. There would be tiny clean islands, ringed with white sand and blue surf, and the air would be warm. In this vision the people were somewhat vague, but they would be lithe, brown, carefree, and they would dance. I didn't know then that millions of other Americans were experiencing exactly the same emotion, as the hula craze and movies like *Bird of Paradise* and a few score Hawaiian bands spread the vision broad and wide.

A cold and un-understanding world kept me from leaving at once for the South Seas, so I turned to the library. The vision grew deeper. In Melville's *Typee* I read for the first time of Fayaway who became the model for endless South Sea heroines: abandonedly voluptuous, a skin "the color of *café au lait,*" a magnificent figure, a slightly fey and doomed look about the eyes, possessed of a deep tribal wisdom that shone through her eyes. In all the books this beautiful stereotype gave herself willingly to the white man although she knew it would end in tragedy.

Lord Byron, something of a connoisseur of women and of love, wrote a book called *The Island* and made it clear that natural passions could have full expression in these exotic islands. Diderot, the famous French Encyclopedist, wrote a rhapsodic book on Polynesia and argued that the "natural" life was far superior to "civilization." I needed no persuading. I plowed through novels, scientific treatises, biographies of missionaries, good writing and bad writing. It was all like diamond dust against a dull jewel; it ground my vision to a lapidary brightness.

Later I was to learn that Melville knew more about whales than about women, that Byron had never been to the South Seas, that Diderot had blatantly fictionalized the voyages of Bougainville. I was also to encounter the numerous works of the professional, nerveless, hard-eyed debunkers of Polynesia. None of this made any difference to me, nor, apparently, does it make any difference to most others who go to Polynesia. The rebuffs, the savage letdowns, the hard surprises, are many, but seldom is the original vision of Polynesia altered. Indeed, in a strange way, the foreigner's vision of Polynesia has come to transform the reality of the place.

And as far as the rush is concerned, many experts say that Tahiti will be Tahiti for many years to come, jets or no jets.

After all, Stevenson stated that he had arrived here "just in time" before the island was completely ruined and Gauguin was told the good years of Tahiti had passed. Even Captain Cook complained on one of his later voyages that things weren't as good as on his first trip there! As a Tahitian friend of mine says, "Things aren't as good as they used to be—and the truth is, they never were."

If you are trying to make up your mind between various resorts and vacation spas, forget Tahiti. It's not an either-or place—"either we go to Jamaica or Bermuda or Palm Springs or Tahiti." If that's the way you're thinking, skip it, because as the Chinese storekeeper says when he tells you you're crazy in Papeete, "your top-side savvy box no be-longee proper."

Tahiti is unique and in no sense a resort—yet. The five little hotels are primitive; most do not have hot water and none accommodates more than sixty people. The best are probably Les Tropiques and Hotel Tahiti, both in attractive bungalow style on the edge of town. While there are no poisonous reptiles, there are bugs, giant moths, spiders, lizards of every hue, mosquitoes, and big land crabs all over the place, generally in one's bedroom. (I'll never forget the night my wife woke me up to ask me to come in and kill a spider that was in the basin. Grumbling sleepily at the alarmist, constant-burglar-hearing species of female, I got out of bed and went into the bathroom. There I woke up quickly, for in the washbowl was something as large as my fist, twice as hairy, and vaguely resembling Godzilla from a horror movie. "I hope you didn't kill it," said the landlord the next day. "Spiders eat insects, they are our friends, you know." "Kill it, hell," I said, "I jumped back in bed and pulled the covers over my head!")

There are few pre-fab entertainments of any sort for the tourist. After you've taken a tour around the island once (half a day) and spent a day or two over at the beautiful neighboring island of Mooréa, you've just about had it as far as organized sightseeing is concerned. Mount

FRED LYON

Papeete harbor.

Orohena rises dramatically out of the middle of the island up to 7339 feet; if you're in the professional mountain-climbing category you might try scaling it. And some ambitious people hike a couple of days into the rugged interior to see the island's one little lake, Lake Vaihiria.

You can also consume one Sunday and a lot of Hinano beer at the Tahitians' ridiculous and charming version of horse races (the jockeys ride bareback, saronged, and drunk). And you can kill a few nights watching the wild and wooly *tamure* dances in the so-called night clubs. (The Bar Lea in town is the best, and the Lafayette out of town for after-midnight action.) Also you can go over to Les Tropiques or the Hotel Tahiti when the Matson ship comes in for its three-day layover and enjoy one of Tahiti's favorite pastimes: tourist watching. They look so much the same—gray, pale, becameraed, and militantly in pursuit of pleasure. After the luau-type dinner that the hotel gives them, the dancing girls—stars such as Tehura and Choua—come churning out with everything God gave them in exciting motion, and every silver-blue-haired mom's mouth sets in a grim Victorian line of disapproval and every paunchy dad's eyes light up with the recollection of fleshly delights he never had.

But after the first three or four days one realizes that there's really nothing much to do—nothing, that is, that you or your libido don't think up by yourselves. A strange sort of depression often comes over one at this point, a feeling that David Huntington has described accurately in *Tahitian Holiday*.

While completing the last short leg of our tour, we gave thought to what we had learned during this first day on the island. We had seen almost everything that is immediately apparent, and it hadn't taken long. As a result, our reflections were suddenly colored by a strange uneasiness tinged with loneliness. Unfortunately, we didn't have the consolation of knowing we were experiencing the usual reaction of almost every new arrival.

This time-worn, often intense complaint is caused by the contrast between what the visitor has read or heard about Tahiti and what he first sees. He

Papeete. Early morning street scene—looking toward the cathedral.

17

has imagined the island as a modern Garden of Eden, a mystic, almost unattainable symbol blessed by perpetual happiness, sublime beauty, and free handouts, both animal and vegetable. Then he arrives; rejoicing at the absence of wet-nursed tours, he does the usual thing and drives in solitary elation around the island. His overembroidered imagination gives way to the letdown of actuality and of frustrated partial fulfillment; though the promise of beauty has been redeemed; he is aware now that landscape, alone, is not enough. *That's all,* he thinks. *What now?* There is nothing to take up the slack.

In his daydreams he has overlooked the possibilities that the carefree, open-armed *vahine* might be occupied elsewhere or might have the flu; that mangoes can be out of season, or that mosquitoes bite, causing one to itch. No nickel-hungry inhabitants have knocked themselves out because of his arrival and he senses—an effect heightened by the shrouded melancholia inherent in Tahiti's beauty—that he is not essential to the island, or perhaps to anything.

He knows, then, that he is far from home and very much alone; to his vague disappointment is added the loneliness of self-excommunication. And even if he is not one of the many who depart on the first available ship, his mental adjustment is nevertheless often difficult.

The sport fishing is poor compared to that of Mexico or Nassau, there's virtually no water-skiing, riding, tennis, or golf, and the beaches, compared to those of Honolulu or the Virgin Islands, are rocky and second-rate. There are only two swimming pools on the island. There's no public library, or even a stand to buy current American magazines.

There are less than two dozen permanent American residents on the whole island of thirty-five thousand people, and these are hardly of the international, partying, jet-set variety you see in Jamaica or Cannes.

And Tahiti's not cheap; don't expect another Spain or Majorca. My house costs about $620 a month, without the servants. Food and liquor are expensive. Just about everything, except fresh fish, coconuts, and women, costs as much as or more here than in the United States.

And the weather. I hate to come right out and say it can be terrible;

let's just say that if I owned Man-Tan I'd get a branch factory going down here as fast as possible. It rained so much one summer (theoretically the best time to go) that I went home after three months paler than when I left San Francisco.

What, then, is so good about the famous Tahiti? Why did I bawl like a baby when I left last year? Why did I come back this year—and reserve the house for next year?

Part of the magic, of course, lies in the visual. The island *is* beautiful, rain or shine. I've never seen a more breathtaking sight than I did when first sailing through that coral reef and into that toy harbor at dawn with the volcanic mountains springing suddenly out of the sea and clawing up into the clouds. (Arrival by airplane is all right but not quite so staggering.) And the little town of Papeete, while dirty and crowded *is*—sorry, there's no other word—picturesque.

Here's how Herb Caen, the San Francisco *Chronicle*'s brash and brilliant columnist, saw it on his twelve-day visit:

The prototype, the original, of all South Seas ports. Red tin roofs steaming in the damp sunlight, acrid smell of copra along the waterfront, ships from the seven seas tugging at their lines: the great *Monterey*, the *Tahitien*; the *Melanesian*, a sleek Japanese training ship. In the distance the fantastic, jagged upthrust mountains climbing more than 6000 feet, straight out of the sea, the shining sea. And, 12 miles off shore, the enchanted Isle of Mooréa —the original Bali H'ai—outlined against the setting sun, looking like a cathedral smashed by a giant. . . .

Ever since Paul Gauguin, the vision of Tahiti has lurked in the back of men's minds like a grain of sand in an oyster, irritating, troubling, always present, always growing, taking shape finally as a symbol of escape, the last place on earth to run away to, a volcanic retreat from reality to real values: love, laughter, peace and plenty. And so it is, even today. As the world grows harder, as the Strontium 90 falls faster, Tahiti remains soft and warm and welcomes you with a kiss on both cheeks. . . .

If you're a luxury-loving efficiency-minded Westerner, its allure is hard to see at first. There is a certain tackiness, even sloppiness, about Papeete. The traffic is a fierce and endless putt-puttpourri of tiny French cars, sputtering motor scooters and whizzing bicycles. The night clubs are bare, wooden and primitive, and the beaches are sparse—either black sand or coral-encrusted. The girls are straight-backed, straight-limbed and golden brown, but they don't really look like Dorothy Lamour in her prime—and even the best hotel doesn't have hot water. And the rains come and go and come again: hot, drenching tropical downpours that seem to evaporate into steam almost before the drops hit the ground. And yet, in a few days, all these things seem unimportant, as they should. The nerves relax, the tensions ease in a warm welter of laughter, and the ever-present scent of tiare Tahiti, the true gardenia.

And there are flowers everywhere: hibiscus, bougainvillaea, tiare Tahiti, chenille, oleander, frangipani, acacia, lily, burau, red and white ginger, poinsettia, lotus, periwinkle, and many more.

But it's the people who live in Tahiti and the people who come to Tahiti that make for the constant fascination of the place. Every day you sit on the quai at the sidewalk café called Vaima, formerly Vaihiria, and you sip your rum and discuss who slept with whom the night before and watch the never-ending parade of characters.

For example, Émile Gauguin is sure to stroll by; he's the painter's sixty-year-old son, and he can frequently be found signing autographs or posing for tourists' shots. ("Look, I picked up a genuine Gauguin picture when I was in Tahiti!")

Ripley Gooding, in his big hat, strides jauntily by, smiling his good horsey smile and looking exactly like the model for *South Pacific's* planter Émile de Becque; part Tahitian, part Bostonian, he is one of the most active men on the island, and his Lotus Village is one of the better bungalow-type "motels" outside Papeete. (Yes, I'm afraid even motels, as of 1960, have come to the island.)

The French baron, who gave up a château in Burgundy for a grass hut, strolls by hand in hand with his saronged *vahine;* Nancy Rutgers, lovely daughter of writer James Norman Hall, comes from market

staggering under the weight of a tuna fish, and a few feet away Henry Taft, a grandson of the twenty-sixth president of the United States, ties up the small boat he sailed here from Honolulu. Smollin, a distinguished-looking general, late of the Czar's Army, shops in a Chinese store. Over there, in front of the Bar Lea, André Kostelanetz, probably the only prominent musician ever to visit Tahiti, has a local musician cornered, trying to find out why there's no minor-key music on the island, and he is temporarily distracted when a gorgeous Tahitian-Peruvian brunette with the incredible name of Nita Wanamaker ankles by in a Dior dress. She in turn stops to talk to someone more incredibly named than herself, Cambridge Shiu, the Chinese merchant. (The Chinese have been very well established in Tahiti since the first of them were brought here in 1864 to work on cotton plantations, which now don't exist. They own most of the stores, dressmaking, tailoring, and camera shops, plus the big vegetable market and many importing firms. There are approximately ten thousand, and they are increasing in numbers as well as in importance.)

Then over there is the eccentric Hungarian painter who paints only one thing: Mooréa. He's been here for twelve years and all he paints is that island a few miles away. He paints it at dawn, he paints it at sunset, he paints it in the sun, he paints it in the rain. "Why should I paint anything else?" he growls. "It is my conscience."

Eddie Lund, the American who years ago came to Tahiti and did more for recording and assembling native music than anyone else, stops his little car and gets out, his monkey Nanette on his shoulder, his pet piglet Joe Sheppard on a fancy leash. "Joe's had a cold," he says as he puts Vicks up its nose.

Personalities—does this island abound in them! Take my neighbors, for instance. I was talking to one, a bald, bearded fellow who had introduced himself as Bengt Danielsson, anthropologist, and I complained that it had taken me ten whole days to get here by steamship.

"Well," he said in his pleasant Swedish accent, "it took me three months."

23

"How in the world did you come?" I asked.

"Oh," he answered, as though it were a most usual form of travel, *"Kon-Tiki."*

The American millionaire down the beach from my house hates noise, and every dawn his native neighbors' roosters woke him up. So he had his butler buy them all and kill them. Soon a new crop and another and another appeared, and he had these killed also. He still doesn't know that he's the greatest single outlet for the rooster market in all Polynesia.

And the French builder with only one eye has several spare glass eyes, so he leaves them on top of posts at strategic places at his various construction sites and claims that the superstitious natives feel extra supervised and turn in much more work than they would if part of him weren't on the job.

And the Frenchman up the hill who plays the fiddle all night to amuse himself has his choice of two instruments—a forty-thousand-dollar Guarnerius or a sixty-thousand-dollar Stradivarius. And the charming retired Chilean diplomat of sixty who lives in a thatched hut with his monkey, parrot, and beautiful twenty-five-year-old vahine who paints abstract canvasses.

Or meet the Noel Coward trio—a retired Englishman, his attractive Parisian wife, plus the most beautiful Bardot-type sixteen-year-old Polynesian female you ever saw.

There's always something fey going on, it seems. Just a few months ago, for instance, Old Mr. B——, ailing senior member of one of the most prominent pioneer families on the island, felt especially poorly and the family sent word for the doctor in Papeete to come with all speed. The doctor, new on the island, wasn't very familiar with the weird Tahitian road and special skills needed to navigate it. So at a narrow-bridged corner he managed to plow into half a dozen Tahitian pedestrians who had decided to loiter there, causing several fractures of diverse limbs. Cursing mightily, the doctor alighted and began mending the injured, because while he was not sure how sick Mr. B—— was, it was quite clear that here were people who needed medical help urgently.

Meanwhile, while waiting patiently, Mr. B—— expired. Aside from their natural grief, the family was distraught to learn that the only hearse on the island had broken down beyond repair, for there is a strict law here that all bodies must be buried twenty-four hours after death. They had to get the deceased the twenty miles into town to the family vault—but there was an equally strict law saying that corpses cannot be transported in private vehicles. However, it was unthinkable to allow him to be buried out here in a tiny cemetery in the district. So they dressed the deceased in his best suit, put some rouge on his gray face, and between two relatives he was walked to the car and placed in the back seat. There he was propped up in a sleeping position and off they went to town. They passed several gendarmes, but all went well. Then they came to where the doctor had had his accident, and there were policemen hovering about. They looked in the car, but the bereaved smiled and said that their companion, who had slipped to the floor, was drunk, and the police nodded understandingly and waved them on. The deceased was interred in a dignified and impressive ceremony before sunset.

Which leads one to speculate on the grim and disturbing thought: since there is no embalming done on the island and the medical facilities are rudimentary and the authorities demand such a quick burial—how many poor souls have been buried alive? Take the case of one of the natives, another personality. His father was buried not long ago, and a few days later the villagers were horrified to see that his coffin had pushed up through the shallow earth covering and remained at a forty-five-degree angle. At the same time many people fell ill and there were suddenly no fish to be caught. For weeks there were no fish.

"It is the work of *tupapa'u,*" said the witch doctor, "the ghosts." He told the native that his father had cast an evil spell before dying and there was only one way he could break it.

"You must go at night to the cemetery and stab your father."

So at midnight Jacques went to the graveyard and opened his father's

Baron Robert Putigny left a French château ten years ago for a thatched cottage in Tahiti. Here he clowns with what he hopes is a friendly shark.

PUTIGNY

Mrs. James Norman Hall at her charming house on the beach a few kilometers from where the Bounty landed.

Parkin Christian, great-grandson of Fletcher Christian, pays a visit to Papeete from Pitcairn.

LEFT: One of the author's neighbors, Agnes, pronounced Ahnyess, is the only Tahitian painter on the island.

PALACIOS

ta Wanamaker, orig-
lly Teaotea Aunda,
quired her name
rough marriage to an
merican. She rarely
esses in anything less
an Dior costumes.

MACKENZIE

LEFT: *Bengt Danielsson, formerly
of the* Kon-Tiki, *now permanently
of the Paea district.*

CONRAD

27

coffin and stabbed him and blood spurted out. Then they buried the coffin again, people got well, and the fish came back.

"Wasn't it a hard thing to do?" I asked.

He shrugged. "I had to do what the medicine man said. Besides, I hated my father."

The superstitions on this island are varied, imaginative, and rampant, and they are not confined to the Tahitians. I know of several chic and educated white residents who are extremely careful to burn or flush all their nail parings and hair cuttings so that their servants won't use them to cast evil spells on them. And as for stone tikis: every long-time resident seems to have a special story about how so-and-so found a stone image in the back yard and didn't respect it or moved a tiki from one place to another and dropped dead the same day.

"Move a tiki?" exclaimed one svelte American-born matron to me the other day. "Are you crazy? When I want to commit suicide I'll do it a pleasanter way, with cyanide."

Characters, characters. Michener writes in his book *Return to Paradise:*

Tahiti encourages the wacky life. In a world grown exhaustingly serious, here you can observe the rich variety of life. In one day—that's less than sixteen hours—I witnessed the seven following incidents: (1) There was a small riot at the school, more noise than trouble, but a leading businessman who had no doubt often suffered there in his youth jammed on the brakes of his truck, leaped astride the hood and shouted fiercely, "Vengeance! Vengeance! Death to the teachers!" Having provided this vocal support, he got back into the truck and drove off. (2) A woman of forty appeared for dinner at the leading hotel dressed in sneakers, midriff bathing suit and sable overcoat. (3) In a crowd of girls I noticed one with an ugly complexion and strange manner. Finally I asked about her and was told, "That's Jules from Mooréa. He didn't want to be a man so everybody agreed that he could be a woman." (4) At the boxing matches a gigantic bruiser dashed to the middle of the ring and cried, "You have been very patient. All night you

OPPOSITE: *The American who moved this tiki from a neighboring island is said to have dropped dead the same day. (Chronic alcoholism may have helped the tiki gods in their vengeance.)*

MACKENZIE

have waited for a real champion to box. Well, here I am!" At the bell he roared out, swinging like the windmills of Holland. Four minutes and twelve seconds later he was colder than a dead squid. When brought to, he jumped up and bellowed, "I'll be lots better next week." Explained his manager, "We have to keep him likkered up to keep him brave. This time we overdid it." (5) A Frenchman with no money arrived in Tahiti and announced that he was the son of a Viscount. Everyone knew he wasn't, but they humored him. "After all, if he wants to be the son of a Viscount, why not? The funny thing is that after two years, we began to think he was, too." (6) A wealthy man and woman were flying back to Honolulu. Two Tahitian girls said they'd never been up in an airplane and would like to go along. Three weeks later we received the news, "We enjoyed the trip so much we're going on to Paris." (7) The copra crop was bad in Paea and parents hadn't much money for Christmas, so the chief sent word to all children, "It is very sad. Père Noël just died."

And *les vahines*—the women—can be characters too, perhaps the most important characters on the Polynesian scene. Older characters, like the colorful Princess Turia and the completely charming "Lala," widow of James Norman Hall. (I recently saw six men clustering about her at a party while she told an amusing story about her "Jeemey" and made them all forget she wasn't still the beautiful young Tahitian girl Hall married so many years ago.) And the colorful Margaret Curtis, the one-time concert singer who has been commuting between Tahiti and San Francisco for thirty years. And the supposedly older, dignified, and whacky Tahitian matron who came up to me at a party the other day and said in her fascinating accent, "Hey, how come the TEAL plane no fly today?" I answered I thought it had. "No," she said. "Pilot friend of mine—whenever they go, the pilot come over my house when I'm taking sunbath by the pool—he wave his wings, I wave my teets. I think he don' leave today."

And what about the young Tahitian women? Is it true what they say about them?

Captain Bligh described Tahiti as "the finest island in the world . . .

where the allurements of dissipation are beyond anything that can be conceived."

People have been kissing and telling on Tahitian women for centuries. Here's one of the first—and best—evaluations of them written in 1773 by Captain Cook:

Great injustice has been done the women of Otaheite* . . . by those who have represented them, without exception, as ready to grant the last favour to any man who will come up to their price. But this is by no means the case; the favours of married women, and also the unmarried of the better sort, are as difficult to be obtained here as in any other country whatever. . . . On the whole, a stranger who visits England might with equal justice draw the characters of the women there from those which he might meet with on board the ships in one of the naval ports, or in the purlieus of Covent-Garden and Drury-Lane. I must, however, allow that they are all completely versed in the art of coquetry, and that very few of them fix any bounds to their conversation. It is therefore no wonder that they have obtained the character of libertines. . . .

No question about it, most Tahitian women today are more relaxed and overtly delighted by sex than most of our women. But then they're more relaxed about everything in life. And if you walk into some bar like the famous Quinn's on the waterfront you're going to find the most relaxed atmosphere you've ever been exposed to. I won't say it's the roughest joint I've ever been in, but I will say that when I walked into it at high noon for the first time some unidentified vahine gave me the friendliest, warmest, and lowest handshake I've ever experienced. Quinn's, incidentally, used to be a wonderful place. In the thirties and until 1953, Eddie Lund, a Seattle boy who had been an accompanist for Lillian Roth, operated it and played the piano—a great piano—and Bill Stone, the novelist, played the saxophone. They are two of the most

* On his first visit, Cook apparently asked a Tahitian, "What is this island called?" and received the answer, "O Tahiti," It is Tahiti. It was thus wrongly labeled until Bougainville came along.

31

popular Americans ever to visit Tahiti, and people flocked to see them. Then Eddie became *fiu*—a much-used term here meaning fed up—and quit, and Bill was busy turning out successful books such as *Tahiti Landfall* and *Two Came by Sea* and the spirit of Quinn's was gone. Now it is a rough, dirty place where men who travel by ships seek out liaisons with the least attractive girls on the island. Still, on a roaring Saturday night it holds a certain fascination, and every once in a while you will see a truly beautiful girl—maybe a new young girl from the other islands come to Papeete to try her luck—get up and dance a *tamure* that you will never forget. David Huntington, in *Tahitian Holiday,* has captured the strange allure of Quinn's in this lively passage:

Waltzes or slow fox trots are played for a while; people glide sedately around the dance floor or sip, politely watching. They are only waiting.

Then the explosion comes. A beating of tomtoms quickens the pulses, and eyes shine in anticipation. Suddenly the beat is overwhelmed by bouncy, raucous music, impossible to describe—and irresistible. Tables are emptied, and the arena is a pulsating, frenzied mass. *Fonctionnaires* in white, sailors on shore leave, beachcombers, or the well-to-do are converted to and augment the delirium. The girls are mostly native. Many of them have a pagan and sensuous beauty, and each is intensely faithful to her *tane* until she changes her mind. *Vahines* from the outlying islands are there too, completely amoral, drawn by the happy prospect of a well-heeled *liaison,* or at worst (who cares really?) a riotous succession of inexpensive days and nights. From the edge of the dance floor the selection of one of these delightful companions of the night (or year) is facilitated by a judicious, melonlike palpitation of gyrating posteriors. The choice made, a lift of an eyebrow conveys the welcomed message.

Suddenly it is dark. The tables are occupied, and a spotlight throws a smoky cone on the center of the floor. We wait for a volunteer.

"Phaedra!" someone shouts.

"Augustine!" The clamor is taken up by others, and Augustine it is. Quickly, laughingly, she exchanges the lower half of her two-piece cotton dress for a native skirt of rustling fibers.

32

Her diminutive, exquisitely proportioned body is bathed in the pillar of light as it waits for the feel of the music. It is caught. As though her torso has been grasped by an unseen, wrenching hand, her head falls back and her body, seemingly living a life of its own, responds to the beat. Slowly, and then faster and faster, the primitive, joyous invitation unfolds.

As expected, a partner is enticed from the crowd. But this time it is no native *tane* who leaps to her side; instead, a grotesque, ludicrous *popaa*, wearing a novelty-shop Cyranolike proboscis with attached celluloid eyeballs, capers about her like a demented satyr. The crowd loves it and goes wild. With her head still thrown back and her expression one of orgiastic torment, Augustine redoubles her efforts. The popaa stumbles, falls, and passes out at her feet. The timing is perfect: on the last beat of the drums the goldenskinned succubus swoops on the vanquished goblin and unmasks him. . . .

Although the crowd leaves Quinn's when it closes and continues on to the Lido and later to Lafayette (both are mercifully located out of town at the water's edge). Quinn's remains, as it has been through the years, the center of public social life. Unless one has been to Tahiti, the reasons are hard to understand. Barnlike, dirty, and ill-smelling, it offers nothing but the spirit of its *habitués*. The unpartitioned restroom is coeducational and has the physical attributes of a swamp. Ladies dressed in Fath, Dior, or local Chinese originals depart in laughing groups, in a sort of jovial routine, for the nearest bush or dark alley and think nothing of it. Food is unobtainable at Quinn's. . . . Yet Quinn's has something that makes it preferable to the best of its plush-lined counterparts at home. It is the present-day soul of Tahiti, where hearts are light. The great unwashed and the Governor understand this; so does the recent arrival from Chile or the pearl diver from Hikueru. We understood it too, and I loved it.

The reputation for the island women's greatness in the hay is said to be well deserved by some; a prominent doctor studying the customs there told me that it's because of their uninhibited natures and also because of certain interior muscles which the girls develop through those incredible, convulsive dances that they perform from childhood.

33

("Like a man shaking hands," he stated, though somehow it sounded more scientific when he said it.)

However, according to some experts the women do not appreciate love play or any embellishments of the sex act. Some people claim that the dancing takes the place of any preliminaries and that since the average white man doesn't dance the tamure he is bound to have a disappointed partner. Bengt Danielsson's book *Love in the South Seas* is a fascinating scientific treatise on the subject in all its complexity.

Disarmingly, the word for making love is *hauti*, which means to play; there are no words for indecent, obscene, perversion, or illegitimate. It has been estimated that some seventy-five per cent of all the children on Tahiti are "illegitimate," but the Tahitians take no notice of that term. To them a baby is a baby and hence highly desirable. Frequently when a young girl gives birth to a healthy baby several young men will lay claim to being the father. Some sociologists state that the universal love of children is what accounts for the lack of neurosis on the island; children are brought up with large families and have several sets of "parents" in the form of other relatives and friends, and hence are not victims of the jealousies and frustrations of "civilized" families where the love of one set of parents must be shared with siblings. Though there is no cause for shame when an unwed girl has a baby, she frequently gives it away to some relative who has several boys and not enough girls or vice versa.

Whatever their sex life, the girls are friendly and delightful. At first many people are disappointed in their looks; unfortunately, not every girl in Tahiti looks like a tanned Elizabeth Taylor. Many are fine-looking in every other way except in the teeth department, due to the lack of dentists' care and absence of minerals in the drinking water. When you're driving along Tahiti's one road you frequently see up ahead a motor scooter, and astride it a superb nineteen-year-old body dressed in a scanty flowered print, waist-length hair flying in the breeze. You speed up, come alongside, and see that she has the face of a goddess.

You smile. And then she smiles. No teeth! The classic present for a *popaa* (white visitor) to give his vahine when he leaves the island is a dental bridge. One enterprising Hollywood movie company put this deficiency to great practical use; since the girls are notoriously undependable, work only when they feel so inclined, and are not sufficiently interested in money, the producers played on their vanity. They brought a dentist who would fill their oral gaps with bridges. However, the girls had to turn in the false teeth every night before leaving the set, and gained complete possession only when the film was finished.

Of course there *are* girls with perfect teeth and perfect everything, girls so beautiful they make you ache inside, but they are not as plentiful as the travel folders would like to have you believe. Yet, while there are few girls who individually would qualify as classic beauties, collectively they give the impression of beauty. I think the Tahitians have acquired their reputations for pulchritude largely because of their magnificent bodies and hair. Also, the Tahitian girl's skin is usually of a beautiful color and amazingly soft, and her eyes are nearly always lovely. A delightful custom is that the standard form of greeting in Tahiti is kissing—on both cheeks, yet.

James Ramsey Ullman has written of the Tahitian woman that she is the *force majeure* of the island, the very incarnation of the ambiance of Tahiti:

Physically they vary greatly; for the pure Polynesian is today a rare bird on the island and, as likely as not, the so-called Tahitienne will have inherited a different racial strain from each of the four grandparents. Those of preponderantly native blood are likely to run to heft and girth, to a degree rather forbidding to Western tastes. But those of mixed ancestry— called *demis*—are usually far more delicate of frame and feature; and half-Tahitian half-Chinese, in particular, are often (and I make the statement categorically) as beautiful as a woman can be. Fat or thin, however, beautiful or only middling, all short of the old-crone stage have a quality of style. Whether in a Dior replica, *pareu* with garlands, or in blue jeans and her boy friend's sport shirt, I never once saw a *vahine* I would call a frump.

SYLVAIN

*Different styles of
the* tamure *dance.*

PUTIGNY

MACKEN

36

As for their well-known "availability," the answer is that it's as reported. But while the newcomer may be prepared for this, he probably will be surprised by the sweetness and gentility that go with it. There are exceptions, of course. At Quinn's and along the wharves on boat days there are girls as brassily professional as any waterfront tramp. But these are a minority; most are not brassy and most are not tramps. By their own lights they are thoroughly decent and self-respecting *vahines*. And it is their lights, not ours, that make the rule of the road in Tahiti.

Reams of analysis, learned and leering, have been written about Tahitian morality, but it seems to me that the old Ethel Merman song gets to the point quickest and best. It's a matter of "doing what comes naturally." In our Western world society and church, economics and romance have combined to make sex a fearfully complex affair; but to the Polynesian it is no more complex than breathing, eating, sleeping or any of the normal functions of life. In the prewhite world, in which their customs evolved, venereal disease did not exist. And even today, no opprobrium—or problem—is attached to an illegitimate child. Indeed, the very word "illegitimate" is meaningless; for whose laws are we talking about? Surely none that the Tahitian ever dreamed up.

As for communication, it helps if you speak a little French, as almost no Tahitians speak English. The basic tongue is Tahitian, a mellifluous and intricate language. However, the language barrier has been surmounted or ignored in more than one otherwise highly successful liaison. People ask if you have to speak French to enjoy Tahiti; it is like asking whether one has to know French to enjoy France. It certainly helps.

The syndicated columnist Stanton Delaplane recently had an amusing piece on the difficulties that can arise from lack of common language. He called it "Male Call," and in it he solved the problems very neatly:

"Tahitian girl like to dance, drink little beer, go night club, have good time," she said. Her black hair hung to her waist. And her wrap-around pareu was tucked in so carelessly, I thought maybe I should lend her a safety pin.

38

The morning breeze blew softly through the thatch-and-bamboo cottage. And I put a safety pin in my own pareu—I am that modest.

The maid picked up the mop and made a few passes at the polished floor.

She sat down and lit one of my cigarettes. All the maids at Hotel Tahiti drop in for a cigarette in the morning—we hold a little L&M luau.

"You read my letters to me?" she asked.

"With pleasure," I said, getting out my notebook.

There is something about the South Pacific that inspires literary work. It moved Melville to write *Typee*. Loti wrote his *Marriage of Loti*. O'Brien found the pages of *White Shadows of the South Seas*.

I believe all this golden prose was written from golden memory. After they went home. So it seems to be with the departed visitor.

The little brown girl in the little grass shack pulled a sheaf of mail with American stamps from her red-print pareu.

"My dear little girl," said the opening letter, "I am sitting in my New York apartment and dreaming of a black sand beach under the coconut palms . . ."

I do not know the writer. But I know his byline.

He turned up two pages of the fanciest prose I have read in a long time. A good deal better than his last magazine article, I thought.

I read it out for the little brown girl. She nodded all the time in a most satisfied way.

"Very nice boy friend," she said. "Read another letter. . . ."

I asked the lady if she could read her own letters. She said no. "I ask people to read to me. Like you."

It seemed like an interesting sideline to staying at Hotel Tahiti.

The next letter was from a Los Angeles dentist.

"My lonely one," he wrote, "I, too, am lonely. . . ."

A New Jersey insurance man—how did he get down here?—was brisk and businesslike:

"Dear Friend: I took the tube to a shop. They say there is nothing wrong with it. There must be something else wrong with your radio. I am sending the tube back by ship."

"He try to fix radio," said the little brown girl. "*Nice* boy friend."

"Girl must have boy friend for dance, for drink little beer," she said. "Boy

40

friend go back to States get new boy friend. Old boy friend write letter."

I asked her how she answered the letters.

She said she just waited until somebody like me—somebody with a type-writer—came along.

"You write letter for me?"

We sat down and composed some purple prose, if I do say so myself.

"Tell him I very lonely," said the little brown girl.

I put it on pretty good. I told the New York writer that I was combing my long black hair on a black sand beach beneath a coconut tree. I put in enough tropical color to spoil his day.

I gave the dentist enough lonely nostalgia to pull a tooth without anaesthesia.

I told the New Jersey insurance man to cut out the nonsense. "Send me a new radio."

It was a literary triumph. It was also educational. When you get back home from the South Seas, don't write. You may get more circulation than you wish.

One pleasant surprise I wasn't prepared for was the costumes of the men and women—the *pareu* that Delaplane mentions. I had expected the Tahitians to put on sarongs only for ship departures, luaus, and dance performances, as in Honolulu. But in Tahiti the natives dress in the *pareu* (pronounced pah-*ray*-ooh) most of the time. This consists of a wrap-around garment of beautifully designed flowered cloth (made for over a hundred years in Manchester, England). Both sexes wear it, plus a bra to match for the women. Disappointingly, you won't find any girls wandering around without bras, but when you get to know them they'll take them off in a trice when a group of you go swimming in the fresh-water pools up the valleys. They are, however, excessively modest about the lower garment and sometimes never take it off, even when going to bed with a lover.

A less pleasant surprise was the noise of Tahiti. Somehow one doesn't expect Tahiti to be a noisy place. There is the incessant sound of a *toere*—the hollow log used in the Tahitian music—the *swish kerflonk* of falling palm fronds, the plain *flonk* of falling coconuts, the harsh squawk of the omnipresent myna birds, the perpetual boom of the surf on the reef, the shrill beep-beep of *le truck,* the sputterings of myriad motor scooters, the squeal of tires as Renaults dodge squealing pigs, the flopping of giant moths on the window, the rustling of rats in the thatched roofs, the whistling of the wind *maramu* when it's blowing, the barking of dogs, and the crowing of the roosters—nearby roosters, medium-distanced roosters, and horizon-type roosters, but all endowed with the loudest lungs God ever gave poultry.

Incidentally, why someone isn't killed daily by falling coconuts, I will never know. Andrea Balman, one of the top doctors on the island, herself a Tahitian, says she has never heard of anyone being killed or seriously injured by one, yet they fall continually and frequently where someone has just been. One can always recognize newcomers to the island by their failure to park their cars away from coconut trees.

And the way you term "the grapevine" is *radio cocotier*. Someone will say "Radio cocotier says that so-and-so is sleeping with such-and-such."

And to finish up the subject of coconuts, you know you're becoming a real resident of Tahiti when you can skillfully ricochet the big nuts off the road with the side of your tire without even slowing down.

Now to the subject of the natives themselves. And apropos, J. C. Furnas has some wry comment in his fine book *Anatomy of Paradise:*

Positively, the meaning of "Native" can be approximated. It means: Darker. Productive of quaint handicrafts. Given to diving after coins thrown from a ship's rail. Greedy for beads, red calico, silk hats and alcoholic drinks. Suspect of cannibalism. Addicted to drumbeating and lewd dancing. More or less naked. Sporadically treacherous. Probably polygynous and simultaneously promiscuous. Picturesque. Comic when trying to speak English or otherwise ape white ways. Or, to define by example: a "Native" is what

Robinson Crusoe feared had made that footprint. When he turned up, Friday was a "Native" right enough; so was Melville's Queequeg; so was Tondeleyo, who made "mammy palaver" temporarily part of the American language. The "Natives" are badly spoiled . . . the "Natives" are dying out . . . the "Native" dances are wonderful, but you have to get away from towns to see the real thing . . . he went "Native" . . . the "Native" women aren't so much, but the "Native" babies are the cutest little things you ever saw. . . .

Nor can the word be left at that. In reaction against the colonial or globe-trotting snob, the sentimentalist has reversed the onus and vested the poor devil of a "Native" with an aura of pure moonshine. To him anything "Native" is by definition morally, aesthetically or technically superior to any-thing non-"Native," however that would be defined. He shakes his head sadly at the privy that whites force the Native to build, not because it spoils the view or usually defeats its sanitary purpose, but because it is non-"Native" not to defecate on the beach or in the bush. He often insists in print that, by sheer loving-kindness, he succeeded in making fast friends with the Natives and lived among them for months as one of themselves. Never mind if experienced and sympathetic scientists deny that such a psy-chological and physical feat is possible—the Nativephile says he has done it and for the rest of his life preens himself on the accomplishment.

The Tahitian natives are the cleanest people I've ever seen. They generally bathe in the fresh-water streams three times a day. There is never any odor about them, even in the tiny bars where dozens of sweaty dancers are writhing to the frantic beat of a tamure drum; if your nose is ever offended, look around—it's generally an American or a Frenchman.

The smells of Tahiti are varied and fascinating. The exotic smell of frangipani blends with the pungent sweet odor of drying copra; the fruity fumes of a Chinese all-purpose store mix with the scent of new-mown lawn; the iodine stench of bleached coral mingles with the ro-mantic vapors of vanilla, papaya, limes, and baking breadfruit. One

A Tahitian girl does her laundry in a stream. (Photo: Air France.)

smells Tahiti even before landing. As Eugene Burdick wrote in *Holiday* magazine recently:

There is another aspect of the Pacific which, for reasons I do not fully understand, is almost never remarked in writing. That is the smell of the Pacific. In America we have deodorized our culture and our land. Fertilizers are nonorganic and hence farmlands odorless; factories such as breweries and bakeries, which used to give out a great redolence, now have their smells snatched up by blowers and either absorbed chemically or shot high into the sky. And so it goes with almost every smell of America. It is tamped down, obliterated, extinguished.

In the Pacific all of this changes. Things smell. Some of the smells are fundamental, vast, seductive and exciting. Others are shocking and almost beyond the capacity to endure, though one does endure them and finally even ignores them.

There is, first of all, the great emanation that comes from the Pacific itself, for the sea has an odor. It is made up of iodine, algae, dried salt water and occasionally the sharp smell of fresh water on hot flat salty water when a rain squall passes. Coolness itself, you discover in the Pacific, also has an odor: slight, elusive, pleasant. Let a passing cloud or a puff of wind drop the temperature a few degrees, and the difference makes itself felt first of all as an undefinable odor.

Then there is the smell of land. This is the smell of ancient vegetation, tropical plants, and the rind of the sea—mollusks, crabs, mussels, seaweed, tidewater flats, mud. It is a fume that reaches far out from land. In the old sailing days, when sailors traveled on ships which themselves were rank with too many men in jammed quarters and with no water for bathing, the first smell of land was invariably pleasant. Today, for different reasons, it remains so.

As you get closer to shore the thin general odor is replaced by the more solid individual odor of the land you are approaching. This is a more heavy, acid, and sometimes tantalizing smell. It is as if the land projected its personality far out to sea.

The Tahitians are a dignified, friendly, independent, and happy people, but basically very lazy. Why not be? They have everything

OPPOSITE: *Carrying pigs to the Papeete market. (Photo: Mackenzie.)*

they want. There are fish in the sea, and bananas, oranges, breadfruit, and coconuts in the trees. Leave the worry and striving for the crazy popaas and the Chinese.

The Tahitians want almost nothing that they can't get from nature, and this has driven more than one European crazy. Movie companies have frequently given up in disgust halfway through filming a picture because the natives suddenly get *fiu* (fed up) with work and wander off. No amount of monetary offers can get them back until they feel like it. The main reason they work for money at all is to get enough Hinano beer to get drunk on the week end. They don't drink during the week, but come Saturday the whole family is usually off on a party that lasts till Sunday night. They are amiable drunks who just love a good outdoor party with their friends where they laugh and sing and dance and barbecue and let off steam. As Ben Masselink once wrote:

I have often wondered why Maugham wrote much about Samoa but little about French Oceania. I believe it is because for the most part there is no fiction on Tahiti. There is no guile. In rigid, prudish Samoa, like rigid prudish most every place else, desires smoulder beneath the surface and often explode. There are no explosions of this sort on Tahiti, for no steam builds up. The escape valve is candour—Tahitians tell you everything at once. There is no suspense, so no story. Take Maugham's *The Letter*—here there would be no murder—all three, the wife, her husband and the lover, would get together over a bottle of red wine and talk about it and laugh and then someone would start beating a drum and the dancing would go on until dawn.

The best time of all for them is the Bastille Celebration. This starts on July 14 and is supposed to last a week, but generally drags on for three weeks; the intensity of the mooing of the unmilked cows and the barking of the unfed dogs tells you how long the family's been in town. There are spear-throwing contests, and the men's accuracy is astonishing; they can hit a coconut atop a fifty-foot pole at two hundred feet. There are canoe races and singing and dancing and cock fights.

48

Throwing javelins at a coconut high on a pole.

Dancing, booths, beer drinking, crowds, and games of chance characterize every fête, or juillet, as it is called. Most Tahitians avoid hard liquor, preferring Hinano beer and Algerian wine, but the amounts consumed are prodigious, and many people are taero—*drunk—for a week or more.*

Cockfighting in Paea. The Chinese are usually the heavy gamblers at this "sport," which flourishes on Sundays and during the fête.

But most of all the Tahitians enjoy *les baraques,* the booths made of woven palm leaves along the waterfront. Here they have carnival games of skill and chance and little dance pavilions where they drink and do the tamure dance ecstatically all night and most of the day, loving each other, loving life, and loving their island.

Does it all sound too pat, too platitudinous, too traveloguey, this picture of the happy native in the Garden of Eden as the sun sets behind a silhouetted palm frond? I keep looking for the catch but I can't find any; I'm afraid that they are the happiest people on earth in the loveliest setting left to the modern world.

James Ramsey Ullman has written of the Tahitian:

It is on the record, plain and grim, that for some two hundred years, he has been plundered, corrupted and victimized by the white man. And there are those who contend that, beneath the surface, he is sad and lost; awash in a world he never made or asked for, and knowing himself doomed to racial extinction. If this contention is true, however—and it is highly debatable—he is assuredly the world's Pagliacci *par excellence.* Whatever his past and future, he gives, today, an impeccable performance as the happiest of men.

Yes, it's great—for them. But the modern man doesn't always fit in this environment; even back in 1774 George Foster wrote in *A Voyage Round the World:* "It is certain, at the same time, that being born and bred up in an active sphere of life, acquainted with numberless subjects, utterly unknown to the Tahitians, and accustomed to extend his thoughts to past and future occasions, he would shortly have been tired of an uninterrupted tranquility and continual sameness, suited only to a people who are simple and confined." It's nice to think of going back to nature in theory, but that fed-up guy on the Madison Avenue treadmill who thinks he yearns for Tahiti usually can't take it for very long once he gets there. Tahiti tells you who you are quicker than any place I know; it's interesting to see how different people react to the revelation. Thoreau said, "A man is rich in proportion to the number of things which he can afford to let alone." You don't have much of a choice down here—you're forced to do without things you take for granted in America. The guys who find a vahine and a little thatched cottage on the lagoon and "settle down to do some stock-taking and really live" don't seem to stick it out very long unless they have a lot of inner resources. They generally take to the booze pretty hard, and then one day after a few weeks they quietly leave for the familiar frantic pace again, there to dine out on tales of Tahiti, the "place where they *really* know how to live."

In the transition period from rat-race man to confirmed Tahiti lover, the worst time seems to be about the third week. The astonishment over the physical beauty has begun to wear off, you've done all the obvious things, met all the girls, and you begin to get itchy for a play or a newspaper or a book store or a nice new Hollywood movie. That's when the long-time residents of the island look wise and say, "Three weeks in Tahiti is too long, and three months is too short."

As Robert Keable wrote in *Tahiti, Isle of Dreams* back in 1925, it is not Tahiti's fault; it is rather the tourist who is found wanting.

But I leave, and I shall not come back. For the last time I shall see the sun set in all its indescribable unearthly beauty behind Moorea. But I am under no delusion. It is I that have been tried and found wanting. It is I that am outcast for ever from the real Tahiti and dare not insult her again by my return. . . . There I have learned the bitter truth. I belong to the "harshness and hideous sights, and ugly people, and civilization, and corruption and bloodiness, and all evil." I do not belong here. I cannot become a child again and be born anew in this house. It would welcome me as a guest, but I do not want that and I never can become an heir. Not now in all the world shall I ever lift the veil or learn the secret of it! Here is peace; here is beauty as a golden ladder up to the far and unknown heaven of our hope; here is simple, quiet living, boundless wealth, a sure reward. In a thousand islands it is here, and Tahiti keeps the door. But I go. I must have people and self-complacent civilization—and London, I suppose.

But ironically, he wasn't able to leave after all. He is still there, for he found he had tuberculosis, could not return to England, and subsequently died in the Tahiti he loved.

How does an average day go by in Tahiti? Well, I try to get up fairly early and do a little writing or painting. I say try, because too often I just say to hell with it. (The longer you live here the more often you find that little phrase coming to your lips about anything that involves any effort whatsoever. Only after a while you say it in Tahitian: *Aita pea pea.*) After breakfast is served in the big thatched house by two handsome girls in bright pareus, I slide the big outrigger down the beach to the water (or rather, I wait for the gardener to do it!) and spend the morning out on the lagoon goggle-fishing. The water and the fish are beautiful, but it's tough fishing since the native spear-fishermen have made the fish pretty wary. Incidentally, there are no sharks in the lagoon, but there are plenty of moray eels, some four or five feet long with heads and jaws like those of fox terriers, and they are to be avoided. It seems to me that I see them most frequently in the afternoon around five o'clock.

The reef and the lagoon are constantly fascinating. Here's how Robert Keable described their delights:

As we walk along we find a great fissure split in the reef across our path. Put on water-glasses, kneel, take firm hold and plunge your head beneath the surface. For thirty seconds or so you can gaze into literally and absolutely the fairyland of the children's story books.

Imagine a small window in the dome of St. Paul's. Climbing on the outside of that dome, you push your head through and gaze down. That is what you have done on this reef. For it is hollow. Below are enormous caverns, and this fissure is a hole in the roof of one such cavern. For hundreds of feet the water is shot with light, and you can see—see the unbelievable, the supernatural, the tales of faërie.

Pillars of pink and white and purple alabaster, shot with veins of green and gold and silver, sustain the roof. Far, far down the white sandy floor slopes into the mists of depth. Fantastic castles of coral, battlemented, towered and turreted, lift towards you. Flights of little fish, literally living sapphires or emeralds, dart by. Sapphire or emerald forsooth! There are flights of little fish of every imaginable colour and combinations of colour that any artist has ever dreamed. You will see orange fish barred with blue, and black fish barred with silver, and green fish eyed with scarlet, and square fish and tubular fish and flat fish that drive every last belief out of you, for what power, in the name of human sanity, could have conceived them? There are beasts more lovely than birds of paradise, more hideous than a nightmare. There are beasts there that are *both*, at once, though you may not believe it. There are sea-anemones and sea-urchins as big as footballs, and codfish as big as Grenadier guardsmen, and sea horses as small as shrimps. There are shells with a tremulous wave of beauty a-flutter from them and there are crabs with the faces of politicians. Crabs! Every empty shell contains a crab. There are crabs in shells as small as a seed or as big as my head. And the thirty seconds are up now, which is well, for already you do not believe the half that you have seen.

Overwritten? No, understated.

After swimming comes lunch, and what a lunch it can be: marinated tuna (*e ia uta*, or *poisson cru* to the Tahitians), or parrot fish, the freshest lobsters, giant grapefruit (called *pamplemousse* and introduced by botanist Harrison Smith) and avocados, breadfruit, yams, taro, fried bananas, and best of all *poe,* the arrowroot dessert (which has nothing whatsoever to do with that mucilaginous Hawaiian paste called *poi*). The food all over the island is generally surprisingly good, I suppose because of the French influence.

I'd better give you the recipes for both *poisson cru* and poe:

POISSON CRU (RAW FISH)

Use *fresh* fish, meaning caught that day or the night before. The Tahitians use bonita or tuna, but if you can't get either, settle for swordfish or salmon. Cut the fish into very thin one-inch-long strips. Sprinkle the fish with lots of lime juice (fresh) and marinate for one hour. When done, rinse out the juice with water. Spice fish with salt; mix fish with one tablespoon oil and one tablespoon vinegar. Place the fish on a bed of lettuce surrounded with sliced tomatoes. Pour over it one cup of coconut cream (*mitihare*) for every two cups of fish. Sprinkle with shredded carrots, shredded large white onions, and grated coconut. Serves four.

MITIHARE (COCONUT CREAM)

Buy three or four fresh coconuts at your market. Break the nut, pour out the water, grate the flesh. Strain the juice out of the gratings through a cloth. This is mitihare. Do not put in the refrigerator or the fats will solidify.

Mitihare is used in nearly every Tahitian dish—in white sauces, as bases for cake icing, in puddings, ice cream, and raw fish. Good frozen coconut cream can be bought at gourmet shops or Trader Vic restaurants.

BANANA POE

Mix two cups puréed bananas with one cup arrowroot made into a paste with water. Add one tablespoon lime juice, two tablespoons sugar, one-half teaspoon vanilla, and one tablespoon creamed butter. Put in a flat baking dish. Bake in oven for three-quarters of an hour at 350 degrees. Cut mixture into one-inch squares and mix with one cup mitihare. Spike with one teaspoon rum and one teaspoon sugar. Serves four.

PAPAYA POE

Same procedure as above, but cook papayas before puréeing. Add two tablespoons brown sugar and one tablespoon butter. Cool before adding coconut cream.

After lunch you read or take a nap or drive into town to check the bi-weekly mail arrival and see who's new in town. Usually there's a fellow writer on his way through, the most recent being Graham Greene (didn't like Tahiti much), Eugene Burdick (liked it), James Ramsey Ullman (loved it), and Alec Waugh (mad for it). Tahiti's so small that it's hard to miss meeting any personality who comes through, though the Tahitians themselves are completely unimpressed with success and successful people; someone remarked the other day that the only two people in the whole world who could cause a stir in Tahiti would be General de Gaulle and Tino Rossi, a long-time popular Italian crooner whose records the Tahitians love. Even Marlon Brando wandered around the streets of Tahiti only occasionally noticed and never pestered, except by tourists.

After you've cased the town and shot the breeze at a sidewalk café, if you have the energy you can drive out with a girl through the lush countryside, so lush and fertile that—honestly—even the fence posts sprout and turn into trees. And then you stop at a fresh stream in the greenest valley you ever saw. The waterfalls look pretty much the way they did in those old Dorothy Lamour movies, and, if you've chosen well, so does the girl, and how you spend the rest of the afternoon is up to you. To wind the day up you can, if you've a mind to and the mosquitoes don't get too bad, cut a bamboo rod, use your pareu as a net to catch some shrimp for bait, and then snag a few *nato*, a scrappy and delicious troutlike fish. Pull down a breadfruit from a tree, build a fire, and broil your fish while you roast the breadfruit in the coals. There are bananas and oranges for the grabbing, and the girl will show you how to open a coconut. Then you can just sit there lazily hour after hour, engaged in one of Tahiti's favorite pastimes—Mooréa-watching. Mooréa is a fascinating island not only because of its lonely primitiveness, which you can feel when you're actually on it, but because of its strange and mystic physical aspects seen at a distance. Someone once remarked that it looked as though two giant dragons locked in mortal combat had suddenly become frozen and petrified—here a bit of claw juts up, here the swell of a scaly hump, there a terrible jaw. And yet

OPPOSITE: *The* Wanderer *off Mooréa. Though it is hard to believe, the* Bounty *was seven feet shorter than this ninety-eight-foot schooner.*

on another day it will look like two lovers embracing. Michener wrote of its variety in *Return to Paradise*:

Nothing on Tahiti is so majestic as what faces it across the bay, for there lies the island of Mooréa. To describe it is impossible: It is a monument to the prodigal beauty of nature. Eons ago a monstrous volcano exploded and the northern half sank into the sea. The southern semi-circle remained aloft, its jagged peaks looming thousands of feet into the air. From Tahiti, Mooréa seems to have about forty separate summits: fat thumbs of basalt, spires tipped at impossible angles, brooding domes compelling to the eye. But the peaks which can never be forgotten are the jagged saw edges that look like the spines of some forgotten dinosaur. They stand together, the peaks of Mooréa, forever varied, forever new. I once watched them for thirty days, at dawn, at sunset, in the heat of the day, and they showed an infinite variety. They were only nine miles across the bay, but in a storm they would seem to be at the very edge of the horizon. At dawn the orange sunlight made them angry ghosts. At dusk lingering shadows made them quiver in the sky. They reached into the air and pulled down clouds; they dressed in gold and purple. If Tahiti boasted of nothing more than these faery silhouettes across the bay, it would still be one of the most fortunate of islands.

Everyone must go to Mooréa, even if for only a day. You can catch the small launch, crowded with babies, oil drums, bicycles, and people, down the quay and make the two-hour trip for about three dollars each way. It is a visual experience never to be forgotten. Here is traveler Ben Masselink's description of it:

The boat was so crowded that the Captain was nearly pushed over the side. He had to lean way out to starboard and steer with his feet. He had one arm around a small, seasick Chinese boy whom he was trying to comfort.

This crossing can be rough but today the sea was quiet and it was hot. It was pleasant to be on the water again. We watched the different attitudes of Mooréa, watched her get closer, watched her architecture change. The peaks came up and disappeared. On some of the ridges the peaks and needles

"*If Tahiti boasted of nothing more than these faery silhouettes across the bay, it would still be one of the most fortunate islands.*"

and cones had the bubbling black fudge look of the old volcano again flaming to life. The boat caught fire and the captain smiled and shrugged. The exhaust pipe had burned through the asbestos covering and the wood on the cabin top was sparking and flaring up. A man casually leaned over the gunwale, scooped a bucket of sea water and doused out the fire.

We passed a flat section of land, all coco palms, like an atoll, made the reef entrance and glided along in the clearest water we had seen since the Bahamas. Pure white sand bottom, brownish coral heads and the red and green flash of parrot fish. We stopped briefly at a small dock where kids played in the water with bright plastic swan floats and beach balls, their Christmas toys. We skirted the white beach, heading west, and then we rounded a point and there it was.

I gasped. Jo gasped. Mr. and Mrs. Miserable gasped. Paopao Bay. It was the most spectacular thing we have ever seen. You know how Yosemite makes you feel when you get up early in the morning and the sun is just on Half Dome? Or the way Monument Valley looks in the moonlight? That sense of awe. That feeling that there is something great going on. Paopao Bay was ten times Yosemite, ten times Monument Valley, ten times the Grand Canyon. All green and blue, all high and crazy. All around the flat blue mirror of the bay the green needle peaks leaping to the clouds. It was almost too much to handle all at once.

One of these needle peaks has a hole in it and you would swear that God, or somebody an awfully lot like Him, is watching you through that hole. Sputtering into that quiet bay, seeing these peaks and green wedges, the watching land, the white birds against the palms, you can easily understand why the Tahitians worshiped tikis, for Mooréa is the meeting place of the peaks, the tikis, the Gods.

If you feel fancier, you can come back out of the wilds of either Tahiti or Mooréa, clean up, and go to a cocktail party; it seems as though there's one a night around Papeete. Then there are a couple of good little modest restaurants in town (Chapiteau's and Waikiki are the best for French and Chinese cooking, respectively) and after dinner you can be off to the Lafayette night club for some of that great dancing. Or if you're hardy, you can take in a movie at one of Papeete's two theaters, where the film vintage is usually twenty years old at least (a recent big event was the first showing here of *Gone with the Wind*). Rats run under the seats, and the Tahitians get terribly excited and yell obscenities at the villain, since nothing can persuade them that the happenings on the screen aren't actually occurring, but it's an experience that shouldn't be missed. (The Tahitians' favorite actor is Roy Rogers, which they pronounce "rowah roshay." I suppose he should be added to the list of people who could shake up the Tahitians if he suddenly appeared on the island.)

And so the days go by. If you make it through the first restless periods, little by little the great peace of the place will filter into your being; you will forget the inconveniences, you will lose interest in the outside world, the doings of politicians, the machinations of countries, the affairs of starlets, the grim statistics of Labor Day highways. As you sit sipping a rum drink on your lawn under the palms, the smell of frangipani blossoms in the late-afternoon air, the ever-present sound of guitars and rhythmic *toeres* being played in the background, you look across that lagoon, soon to be fireflied by the torches of the fishermen, and the omnipresent clouds of Mooréa start to go red and yellow and green—such a soul-stirring sight that it even makes you forget that some clouds in some countries are mushroom-shaped.

Any man who tries to describe a Tahitian sunset is a fool. The evening sky in general thumbs its nose at description—the stars in this dustless, smogless, cloudless atmosphere are as large and well defined as those in a planetarium.

There is in the air a strange, pervading peace of mind, an absence of urgency, the removal of the weight of our tomorrows, the lack of striving. We Americans don't realize how we strive; day and night, week ends and vacations, at work or play—socially, sexually, and careerwise we never stop striving. Here the people savor *today*, they relish the moment, they forget the future, they relax and wallow in the infinite delights of nature around them.

This, then, is the allure of Tahiti—the past, the present, the eternal allure; this is what the island has to teach us, us of the "civilized" world.

And yet we leave it. "All popaas leave Tahiti sooner or later," say the Tahitians. "They leave weeping, but they leave."

Listen to Rupert Brooke:

I was sad at heart to leave Tahiti. But I resigned myself to the vessel, and watched the green shores and rocky peaks fade with hardly a pang. I had told so many of those that loved me, so often, "Oh yes, I'll come back—next year perhaps, or the year after that—I suppose." I had begun to believe it myself. It was only yesterday, when I knew the Southern Cross had left me, that I suddenly realized that I had left behind those lovely places and lovely people, perhaps forever. I reflected then there was surely nothing else like them in this world, and very probably nothing in the next, and that I was going far away from the gentleness and beauty and kindliness, and the smell of the lagoons, and the thrill of that dancing, and the scarlet of the flamboyants, and the white and gold of other flowers; and that I was going to America, civilization, and corruption, and bloodiness, and all evil. So I wept a little, and very sensibly went to bed. . . .

And Somerset Maugham has said something of the same sort:

The breeze was laden still with the pleasant odours of the land. Tahiti was very far away, and I knew that I should never see it again. A chapter of my life was closed, and I felt a little nearer to inevitable death. . . .

OPPOSITE: *Thatched-roof dwelling inside the lagoon at Punaauia. (Photo: Erwin Lang.)*

*The typical sailing canoe or pirogue of Bora Bora,
preparing for the races at Tahiti.*

OPPOSITE: *Perhaps this photo looks contrived, but
it is a common enough composition around the
fifty-kilometer mark—a vaa on the beach framed by
drying nets in the foreground, a stretch of languid
lagoon, and an uninhabited dream island in the
middle distance.*

65

Dusk and night fishing off the island.

OPPOSITE: *One rarely sees the graceful sailing* vaas
until the July fête *when they are raced. Bora Bora
traditionally has the finest sailors.*

67

PART 2

The indescribable sunsets, the unspeakably beautiful lagoons, the lush and fertile countryside, the crabs and wild boars, the birds and fish—and the people. How did this primordial Garden of Eden become Great Tahiti of the Golden Haze? Where are its beginnings?

Where the real history of Polynesia begins can be recounted only in terms of myths and stories—and by the hard digging of archaeologists. But the creation of "modern" Polynesia is more easily traced first by going to the records of explorers and early voyagers. Even so, there are many contradictions and confusions. Because of the lack of accurate written records and the problems of the many-named Tahitian leaders, the definitive history of Tahiti may never be written.

However, here is an outline of some of the facts that we do know:

1. Modern Tahiti's history begins with its discovery in 1767 by the British navigator Samuel Wallis, who named it King George III Island.

2. Eight months later the French navigator Louis Antoine de Bougainville arrived and named the island "Nouvelle Cythère."

3. Captain Cook landed in the ship *Endeavour* in 1769; he called the island Otaheite, the windward islands the Georgian Islands and the leeward the Society Islands ("Because they lie contiguous to each other" as he wrote).

4. In 1772 the Spanish navigator Captain Domingo Boenechea arrived from Peru. During his second voyage, 1774–1775, he established a colony at the end of the island at Tautira, consisting of two missionaries and a servant.

5. In 1788 Captain Bligh in the H.M.S. *Bounty* sailed into Matavai Bay to collect breadfruit trees, which were intended ultimately to provide inexpensive food for the workers in the West Indies and Jamaica.

6. In 1789 occurred the most famous mutiny of all time.

7. The first London Missionary group arrived in 1797.

8. The first Catholic mission was established in 1837.

9. In 1842 Admiral Abel Dupetit-Thouars took possession of the island in the name of France.

10. In 1880, King Pomare V ceded Tahiti outright to France, which has held the possession ever since.

That is Tahiti's history in a nutshell. It looks simple in outline, but let us take a closer look at the complex sub-plots of the saga.

Not until the sixteenth century did the Pacific Ocean become part of the known world. Through the efforts of early explorers—including Christopher Columbus—to find a route to the West, the vast ocean on the other side of the earth was discovered. In 1513 Balboa from a vantage point near the isthmus of Panama first set eyes on the "quiet" sea, but because this passage was not made usable for nearly four hundred years the route around Cape Horn at the southernmost tip of South America became the shortest one to the great Pacific. Con-

"Captain Wallis meets Purea at the house Agitation."
From an engraving in Hawkesworth's Voyages.

sequently, even after its discovery the ocean drew little attention until the eighteenth-century stirrings of curiosity caused Europeans to voice interest in the immense ocean and peoples that probably existed somewhere "out there."

The first European *known* to land on the island was an Englishman, Captain Samuel Wallis, who, in 1767, claimed the land for King George III. The reception that Wallis and his party received from the Tahitians was anything but friendly, and only after the English made several shows of power—with cannons and swivel guns—was peace made. The natives made several conciliatory offerings, including pigs, cloth, and dogs. Wallis accepted the first two but released the dogs, not knowing what to do with them and not realizing that the Tahitians considered the animals a delicacy.

Wallis and his men disembarked from their ship, the *Dolphin,* at Matavai Bay, which is a short distance from what is now Papeete. This bay, although rarely used by ships today because of the poor anchorage, was in those early days the harbor for most of the navigators who came to Tahiti. The only indication that remains of its importance years ago is a monument to Captain Cook there.

Aside from Wallis's own reports of his discovery, there is the version the Tahitians themselves tell as related by Teuira Henry:*

The ancient native *hi'ohi'o* (seer or prophet) named Pau'e, who was well known in Tahiti, said, ". . . There are coming children of the glorious princess by a canoe without an outrigger, who are covered from head to foot." King Pomare I [prince of Pare], hearing him say so, inquired how a canoe without an outrigger could hold its balance and not upset; so to illustrate his subject, Pau'e took a *'umete* (wooden trough) and set it afloat with a few stones placed in it in a pool of water close by; then turning to the King he said, ". . . It is balanced by its breadth, and so also is the canoe without an outrigger that is coming. . . ."

Three days afterwards, Pau'e died, and a little later the *Dolphin* arrived with Captain Wallis, when the people exclaimed, ". . . There is the canoe without the outrigger of Pau'e, and there are the children of the glorious princess!"

Wallis was received on shore by Queen Purea, who was said to be a great beauty. He was lodged at her home and the hospitality afforded him and his crew was supreme. In fact in the journal kept by one of the crew, George Robertson, is the following note:

July 6, 1767. I was told by one of the Young Gentlemen that a new

* The Reverend J. M. Orsmond was very active in the various islands of the Pacific. He spent the years from 1817 to 1856 for the London Missionary Society in Polynesia and during this time did extensive research and study of the native peoples. His voluminous notes were never published or edited during his lifetime, but his granddaughter, Teuira Henry, undertook this task and was able to present the work *Ancient Tahiti.* Miss Henry lived on Tahiti for many years and was in charge of the mission schools there.

sort of trade took up most of their attention this day, but it must be more properly called the old Trade. He says a Dear Irish boy, of our Marines, was the first that began the trade, for which he got a very severe thrashing for the Liberty. More for not beginning in a more decent manner, in some house, or at the back of some bush or tree. Paddy's excuse was fear of losing the Honor of having the first.

Thus a dear unnamed Irish boy became the very first European to enjoy the delights that were to cause men to extol and dream for hundreds of years.

The only difficulty the Europeans had with the natives was pilfering; the white man's property was in abundance, so why shouldn't they share in it?

A happy atmosphere prevailed, unmarred except for the few moments when the ship's doctor removed his wig in order to wash, and caused a panic among the natives.

Wallis set sail after a little more than five weeks and the island was left alone until the following year when Louis Antoine de Bougainville of France arrived. His two ships, the *Boudeuse* and the *Étoile,* anchored at Hitiaa (you can find the exact spot by driving out to kilometer 34 east). Among the crew were two scholars, an astronomer and a naturalist.

Bougainville knew nothing of Wallis's previous claims to the island, and he took it in the name of France, giving it the charming name of "Nouvelle Cythère"; it recalled to him the small island off the south of Greece, famous as a sanctuary of Aphrodite, where the gods were said to spend their sybaritic holidays. As Bougainville himself described his landing, canoes came out to meet him

full of females, who, for lovely faces are not inferior to most European women, and who as far as beautiful bodies are concerned, could vie with the best in the world. Most of these fair females were naked; for the men and old women that accompanied them had stripped them of the garments which they generally dress themselves in. The glances which they gave us from the pirogues seemed to reveal some degree of uneasiness, not withstanding the innocent manner in which they were given; perhaps because nature has everywhere embellished their sex with a natural timidity; or because even in those countries where the case of the golden age is still in use, women pretend to least desire what they most wish for. The men, who are more simple, or rather frank, soon explained their meaning more clearly. They urged us to choose a woman and to come on shore with her; and their graphic gestures . . . denoted in what manner we should form an acquaintance with her. It was very difficult, amidst such a sight, to keep at their work four hundred young French sailors, who had seen no women for six months. In spite of all our precautions, a young girl came on deck and placed herself upon the quarterdeck near one of the hatchways, which was open in order to give air to those who were heaving at the capstan below it. The girl casually shed the garment she was wearing and to everyone she looked like Venus as she showed herself to the Phrygian shepherd, especially since this girl had the same celestial form of that goddess. Both sailors and soldiers tried to come to the hatchway; and the capstan was never hove with more alacrity than on this occasion.

At last we managed to keep these bewitched fellows in order, but it was no less difficult to control ourselves. One Frenchman, who was my cook, having found means to escape against my orders, soon was returned more dead than alive. He had hardly set his feet on shore with the fair girl whom he had chosen, when he was immediately surrounded by a crowd of Indians, who undressed him from head to foot. He thought he was done for, not understanding what these people were doing, since they roughly began examining every part of his body. After having studied him thoroughly, they returned his clothes, put into his pockets whatever they had taken out of them, and brought the girl to him, telling him to go ahead and satisfy his lusty desires. But all their persuasive arguments now had no effect; they finally had to bring the poor cook back on board, and he told me that I might reprimand him as much as I pleased but I could never frighten him so much as he had just been frightened on shore. . . .*

* From Bougainville's *A Voyage Round the World*.

The kindly reception that Bougainville received was due to the natives' experience with the British. And likewise the principal difficulty the French had with the islanders was pilfering. However, this was more than offset by the mysterious murder of four native men by some of the ship's company. After being approached by their chief, Bougainville endeavored to discover the culprits, and his attitude and personality impressed the brother of the chief so much that the young man accompanied him on his return to France. Perhaps this was the real beginning of the rapport between the French and Tahitians.

Shortly after Bougainville's departure, war broke out between the districts of Pare and Ha'apape in the north and Papara in the south. Chief Amo and his wife Purea, the chieftess who had treated Wallis and his company so well, were overthrown. The young man who came to power, the Prince of Pare, Tu, was to be the founder of one of Tahiti's most important ruling families. He was to become King Pomare I of Tahiti and its dependencies; but at this time he was merely the chief of a minor district which happened to contain the best bay, Matavai, for visiting ships.

About this time, Captain Cook arrived on the first of three voyages he was to make to the island. Wallis's discovery had aroused much curiosity among the English who had organized this scientific expedition to Tahiti. From Wallis's reports it appeared to be in an excellent geographical position for observing the passage of the planet Venus across the sun.

Among Captain Cook's group of scientists was the naturalist Joseph Banks, who had come to study the flora and fauna of the island, and the astronomer Green, who was to make meteorological observations. One observatory was set up at Matavai and another on Mooréa, which Wallis had called "the Duke of York's Island." After a stay of ninety days, during which time the astronomical observations seemed to be very satisfactory, Cook sailed on, accompanied by Tuapia, a dethroned high priest of Purea, who wanted to adopt European ways.

The white man in these early visits brought to the island several virulent diseases that were the original undermining forces in the devastation of the Tahitian population, once estimated at 200,000 and now numbering around 50,000.

The year before Captain Cook was to return to Tahiti, Captain Domingo Boenechea of Peru arrived and named the island "Isla d'Amat." His first act was to shoot four of the ship's company who had been sentenced to death for infractions during the voyage. A fifth escaped to the island. This man, probably the first European to settle on Tahiti, became a member of the high chief Vehiatua's family.

In 1773 Cook returned, and on his departure this time was joined by Hiti-hiti, a young man who remained in England three years before returning to the island. While in England he learned to read and write and became the first native to apply the English script to Tahitian.

The next year, Boenechea made a second visit to Tahiti, bringing along two priests who remained as missionaries. As he was preparing to set sail in January 1775 he suddenly died. He was buried with full religious rites, which caused great curiosity among the natives. His grave was covered with a red blanket and then strewn with branches. When the Spanish had left, the natives took the blanket, only to find it full of fleas—hitherto unknown on Tahiti—which increased and spread throughout the entire island.

The following year, the Spanish returned with provisions for the missionaries, who by that time felt their work to be so unsuccessful that they decided to return home.

In 1777 Cook made his third and last voyage to his "Beloved Island." By this time, Tu's family and the other natives had grown fond of him, and the ship was greeted by all the islanders, who bared themselves to the waist as a token of respect and friendship. The Europeans, asked to reveal themselves similarly, complied only to the extent of removing their hats. Cook was never to return to Tahiti, for two years later he was senselessly killed by the natives of the Sandwich Islands.

Eleven years passed before another European set eyes on the island; the *Penrhyn* visited Tahiti, and one of its officers was a Lieutenant Watts,

Captain James Cook.

formerly a member of one of Cook's expeditions. He was received grandly by Tu (Pomare I), then still king, who produced a drawing of Cook for him. After a brief stay, the lieutenant continued on his voyage to China.

Three months later saw the arrival of a ship destined to figure in one of the greatest sea stories ever told. The HMS *Bounty*, commanded by William Bligh, was commissioned by King George of England to procure breadfruit trees from the island as an inexpensive food to be introduced to the slaves of English planters in the British West Indies. The assignment was simple enough, but this lone ship's arrival and ensuing events have contributed much of the island's fame as a singularly alluring phenomenon of beauty—a Circe among islands. Consequently, and since many people think immediately of the *Bounty* when Tahiti is mentioned, largely because of Nordhoff and Hall's fictionalized trilogy and the films

77

based on it, the familiar story of the mutiny is perhaps worth recounting in some detail.

C. S. Wilkinson wrote in his book, *In the Wake of the Bounty,*

although she won no victories, brought home no treasure, and her end was ignominiously to be burnt by men of her own crew . . . yet [the *Bounty*'s] fame is secure, for one April morning in 1789 as she sailed homewards through the islands of the Pacific, there took place on board her what men have agreed to call the greatest of mutinies, led by the greatest of mutineers. Moreover, this was followed by one of the most famous of open-boat voyages; by a trial, death sentences, and pardons; by a romantic settlement on a desert island; and about the whole affair in general, and its leading character in particular, is an attractive atmosphere of mystery.

Fletcher Christian, our leading character in this tale, came from a politically and socially prominent family in Cumberland, England.* There is scant information concerning his early years; Isaac Wilkinson, a close friend and poet of some local prominence, had this to say about him:

> His soul was open, generous and humane:
> His was a heart that felt for others' pain;
> Yet quick of spirit as the electric beam
> When from the darkling clouds its lightnings gleam.

It was the desire of his family that Christian assume the responsibility of the family estate, since his five brothers had been educated for the professional life. But in 1781 Fletcher Christian, then eighteen years of age and filled with a craving for the sea, crept through a window of his home, dropped to the ground, and set off in the direction of the port of Whitehaven, where he shipped out on a voyage.

* I am ridiculously proud of the fact that Fletcher Christian's first cousin, Thomas Law, married my great-great-grandmother Eliza Custis, granddaughter of Martha Washington.—B.C.

His brother Edward gives this account of the young man at this time:

Christian, having stayed at school longer than young men do who enter the navy, and being allowed by all who knew him to possess extraordinary abilities, is an excellent scholar, and everyone acquainted with him from a boy till he went on board the *Bounty* can testify that no young man was ever more ambitious of all that is esteemed right and honourable among men, or more anxious to acquire distinction and advancement by his good conduct in his profession . . . and he declared to a relation who met him at Woolwich that he had been extremely happy under Captain Courtenay's command, and at the same time observed that *"it was very easy to make one's self beloved and respected on board a ship; one had only to be always ready to obey one's superior officers, and to be kind to the common men, unless there was occasion for severity, and if you are severe when there is just occasion they will not like you the worse for it."* . . . Whilst he was in treaty with a merchant in the city [London] . . . Captain Taubman, a relation of Christian's, came to London from the Isle of Man and suggested to Christian that it would be very desirable for him to serve under so experienced a navigator as Captain Bligh, who had been sailing-master to Captain Cook, and who was then in the merchants' service: and as Captain Taubman was acquainted with Captain Bligh, he offered to make an application to him in Christian's favour. The application was made, and Captain Bligh returned a polite answer, that he was sorry he could not take Christian, having then his complement of officers. Upon this Christian of his own accord observed that "wages were no object, [he] only wished to learn his profession, and if Captain Bligh would permit him to mess with the gentlemen, he would readily enter the ship as a foremast-man until there was a vacancy among the officers. . . ."

To this proposal Captain Bligh had no objection, and in that character he sailed one voyage, and upon his return spoke of Captain Bligh with great respect. . . . The captain had been kind to him in showing him the use of his charts and instruments, but at the same time he observed that Captain Bligh was very passionate, yet he seemed to pride himself in knowing how to humour him. In the next voyage Captain Bligh took him out as his second mate, and before his return the captain was chosen to command the *Bounty.* . . .

In view of this tribute and many others that were to come later, one wonders how such a responsible and able seaman could become the leader of the most famous mutiny in history. The circumstances under which the mutiny occurred would have to have been extraordinary.

Captain William Bligh, a Cornishman, was a seaman with a distinguished record at sea and had sailed with Captain Cook on the last of his three voyages to the South Pacific. It has been said that many of his faults can be attributed to his devotion to the state, his employer. However, this fact alone is not enough to mitigate the many criticisms of his character made by naval officers and other public servants (and the interesting fact that years after the *Bounty* mutiny he was involved in another mutiny against him).

In May 1787, Captain Bligh prepared to set sail on his well-outfitted ship. The voyage was undertaken partially at the encouragement of the naturalist Joseph Banks, who had, aside from financial interests in the endeavor, great interest in the flora and fauna of Tahiti which he had studied previously while part of Cook's first expedition. The voyage commenced under favorable weather conditions which soon changed and delayed the ship one month. Bligh was quite naturally upset by this, as it meant arriving at the Cape Horn at an unfavorable time of year. Consequently, he took the power to vary the route of the journey at his own discretion. Fifteen men deserted at Deptford and Spithead. Those who continued on with the ship seem to have been volunteers. Finally, on December 23, 1787, the *Bounty* got under way with a normal crew composed of men of varied temperaments and abilities.

The first indications of trouble arose after the ship had made a brief stop at Tenerife. Bitter accusations regarding stolen food brought threats of flogging; complaints brought reductions in rations. When the daily ration of bread was reduced by two-thirds in hope of making the food last until the ship reached Tahiti, the atmosphere on the vessel worsened.

80

Captain William Bligh.

But Bligh took pride in reporting that when the *Bounty* crossed the Line on February 6, 1788, no cases of sickness had been reported.

On February 17 Bligh wrote to Duncan Campbell, a friend, "My men are all active good fellows, and what has given me much pleasure is that I have not yet been obliged to punish anyone. . . . We now understand each other so well that we shall remain so the whole voyage unless I fall out with the doctor who I have trouble to prevent from being in bed fifteen hours out of the twenty-four."*

On March 19 the first punishment was meted out when the master reported Quintal, an able seaman, for insolence and mutinous behavior; Quintal was given twenty lashes.

* The doctor was clearly ill, since he died later in the voyage.

By early spring the ship had run into more weather difficulties. Bligh's log entry reads:

I was obliged to allot the great cabin, of which I made little use except in fine weather, to those people who had wet berths to hang their hammocks in. . . . With all this bad weather we had the mortification to find, at the end of every day, that we were losing ground . . . we were doing little better than drifting before the wind.

(Fortunately, Bligh kept a full and vivid logbook, even during the terrible and precarious days he spent in the open boat; it was almost as though he foresaw the importance it would have in the future.)

Finally, after thirty days of useless battling with the weather, Bligh forsook the idea of rounding the Horn and headed toward the Cape of Good Hope. The *Bounty* anchored in False Bay on May 24, 1788, and was given a complete overhauling. She remained there for a little over a month and then set sail for Australia; she arrived at Adventure Bay on August 21. On September 4 she set sail once more—but now with open friction developing between the officers and the captain. As she headed for Tahiti, the first casualty of the voyage occurred when James Valentine, A.B., died, probably because of the incompetence or illness of the surgeon.

On October 26, 1788, the *Bounty* reached Tahiti. Like many of the earlier visitors there, Bligh and his crew were given an enthusiastic greeting and the breadfruit trees were soon ordered. However, the trees were not at a stage conducive to transplanting, and this necessitated a longer stay than was first anticipated. The ship remained at Tahiti for over five months—a delay which was to prove the great mistake for Bligh. After their arduous voyage the crew were greatly attracted to the relaxed atmosphere of the island, and discipline became impossible. Most compelling of all was the tremendous allure of the women, with whom many of the men had formed alliances, making the prospect of returning to the *Bounty* so unappealing that on January 5, 1789, three men deserted in a small cutter with arms and ammunition. Blame was put on the petty

Bligh and his crew of the Bounty *received by the Governor of Timor after the 4000-mile trip. Engraving, 1791.*

officer for being asleep at the watch, and he was put in irons as punishment. Nineteen days later the deserters were found and flogged.

Bligh did little during this time to place himself in good favor with the crew, since all the presents and food brought aboard were claimed for the ship.

On February 6 the ship's anchor cable was found cut, and suspicion immediately fell on the natives, who were believed to have been influenced by Thomas Hayward, a midshipman, who was trying to delay leaving Tahiti.

Finally, after preparation during March, Bligh wrote:

We made sail, bidding farewell to Otaheite, where for twenty-three weeks we had been treated with the utmost affection and regard, and which seemed to increase in proportion to our stay. That which followed more than sufficiently proves; for to the friendly and endearing behaviour of these people may be ascribed the motives for that event which effected the ruin of an expedition that there was every reason to hope would have been completed in the most fortunate manner.

After setting sail for home, an incident similar to the one encountered on the first part of the voyage occurred—the officers were accused of stealing food from the captain; but this time Fletcher Christian was made to suffer the captain's rage. The maniacal fury of Bligh repeated itself several times, and each time Christian bore the brunt of the anger. The young seaman began to feel that the situation had become unbearable. Finally, twenty-two days from Tahiti, he prepared to jump ship alone at night on a raft.

Although Christian has been presented as an impetuous, power-hungry hot-head by some writers attempting to whitewash Bligh, it cannot be doubted that he must have found conditions appalling to have been willing to brave the sea and the hostile islands rather than put up with Bligh any longer. The chances of reaching Tahiti, hundreds of miles away, were negligible, the chance of ever seeing England and his family again were poor, and Christian knew it; yet anything was preferable to the captain. His best hope was to drift to some minor island.

That afternoon, Christian gave away all the curiosities he had brought from Tahiti and was seen tearing up letters and other papers and throwing them overboard. He also asked for nails from the carpenter, who told him he could have as many as he wanted from the ship's locker; to the carpenter it seemed a strange request, since the nails could have been of no use to Christian except on land, and the ship was scheduled to stop at no other islands. Robert Tinkler, one of Christian's mess-mates, also remarked later that he went below that evening, feeling hungry and hoping to get some of the pork that was left from dinner, which at first he was unable to find; but after a search he discovered it packed with some breadfruit in a dirty clothesbag in Christian's locker.

84

A re-enactment (1961) of the landing of the Bounty *in Matavai Bay.*

Christian proceeded to build a raft by lashing a plank to the two masts of a launch. But he was unable to leave the ship that day, because many of the crew were on deck watching a volcano on the nearby island of Tofoa. That evening he was invited to dine with Bligh, but excused himself by saying he was ill; the officers agreed among themselves that they would all use this excuse to avoid spending any more time than was necessary with the captain. However, Hayward, now released from irons, broke the agreement.

That night was beautiful, and even Bligh and John Fryer, Master, who

Two motion pictures have been produced based on Nordhoff and Hall's Mutiny on the Bounty. Below is a full view of the ship used in the later version which was filmed in Tahiti in 1961. (SEE ALSO PRECEDING PAGE.) The ship is exact in every detail except that it is ten feet longer than the original. It cost $750,000 to build in Nova Scotia; the original cost: £1950 in eighteenth-century England.

A still from the first movie of Mutiny on the Bounty *released in 1935, starring Charles Laughton as Captain Bligh and Clark Gable as Fletcher Christian. The new film features Trevor Howard and Marlon Brando in these two leading roles.*

were not normally on speaking terms, exchanged comments in a friendly fashion.

At three o'clock in the morning Christian decided that the opportunity for escape had come. A stirring on deck forced him to wait an hour longer, when he would be called for watch duty. At four o'clock, Christian was awakened by Midshipman Stewart to take over command of the deck. He appeared in a "state of some disorder," and Stewart advised him to abandon his project. Christian then went on deck to find Hayward and Hallet, mates of the watch, and found them both asleep. According to his own story, it was then and not before that he abandoned his idea of leaving the *Bounty* and decided to take over the ship.

Once the decision was made, Christian had little trouble getting followers. Before long, there were seven men behind him. They managed to get the key to the arms chest by telling the man in charge that they needed a musket to shoot a shark which they said was alongside the ship.

Captain Bligh recorded his realization of the happenings as follows:

Just before sunrise, while I was yet asleep, Mr. Christian with the master-at-arms, gunner's mate, and Thomas Burkett, seaman, came into my cabin and seizing me, tied my hands with a cord behind my back, threatening me with instant death if I spoke or made the least noise. I, however, called as loud as I could, in hopes of assistance; but they had already secured the officers who were not of their party by placing sentinels at their doors. There were three men at my cabin door, besides the four within: Christian had only a cutlass in his hand, the others had muskets and bayonets. I was hauled out of bed and forced on deck in my shirt, suffering great pain from the tightness with which they had tied my hands. I demanded the reason of such violence, but received no other answer than abuse for not holding my tongue.

The several men who Christian knew would give him trouble were soon arrested. The others learned that Christian's plan was to set Bligh and three other men adrift in a small cutter. But at the pleas of one of the arrested men who knew the boat to be unseaworthy Christian changed his plans and put Bligh in a larger boat—for the sake of the

Seizure of Captain Bligh by the mutineers. Woodcut, 1845.

other men who were to go with him. In the end, after much wrangling and indecision, nineteen men including Bligh were put in the over-loaded boat with limited provisions, leaving twenty-five men on the *Bounty*. Bligh describes the departure:

Notwithstanding the roughness with which I was treated, the remembrance of past kindnesses produced some signs of remorse in Christian. When I asked him if this treatment was a proper return for the many instances he had received for my friendship? He appeared disturbed at my question, and answered with much emotion: "That—Captain Bligh—that is the thing. I am in hell—I am in hell" . . . he seemed as if meditating destruction on himself and everyone else.

Bligh, to the end, continued to cast all the blame for the mutiny on the charms of the women of Otaheite.

The pros and cons concerning the real responsibility of the mutiny are endless. Undoubtedly there are valid arguments that can be made for both the mutineers and the captain. But according to experts who have studied the case there is the feeling that without Bligh's deserved or undeserved unpopularity there would have been no mutiny, and without the lure of Tahiti's women there would have been no mutiny, and even with these two ingredients, the third and most important—the unusual temperament of Fletcher Christian—was necessary to produce the final drama.

It was May 3rd. And for Captain Bligh it was only the beginning. His early plan to stop at a nearby island was abandoned when it was found that the natives were hostile to the men in the launch.

Here is Bligh's own account of the encounter:

After dinner, we began, by little and little, to get our things into the boat, which was a troublesome business, on account of the surf. I carefully watched the motions of the natives, who continued to increase in number; and found that, instead of their intention being to leave us, fires were made, and places fixed on for their stay during the night. Consultations were also held among them, and everything assured me we should be attacked. I sent orders to the master that, when he saw us coming down, he should keep the boat close to the shore, that we might the more readily embark.

The sun was near setting when I gave the word, on which every person who was on shore with me boldly took up his proportion of things and carried them to the boat. The chiefs asked me if I would not stay with them all night. I said, "No, I never sleep out of my boat; but in the morning we will again trade with you, and I shall remain till the weather is moderate, that we may go, as we have agreed, to see Poulaho, at Tonga-taboo." Macca-ackavow then got up and said, "You will not sleep on shore, then, Mattie?" (which directly signifies, we will kill you); and he left me. The onset was now preparing: every one, as I have described before, kept knocking stones together; and Eefow quitted me. All but two or three things were in the boat, when we walked down the beach, every one in a silent kind of horror. We all got into the boat except one man, who, while I was getting on board, quitted it, and ran up the beach to cast the stern-fast off, notwithstanding the master and others called to him to return, while they were hauling me out of the water.

I was no sooner in the boat than the attack began by about two hundred men; the unfortunate poor man who had run up the beach was knocked down, and the stones flew like a shower of shot. Many Indians got hold of the stern rope, and were near hauling the boat on shore; which they would certainly have effected, if I had not had a knife in my pocket, with which I cut the rope. We then hauled off to the grapnel, every one being more or less hurt. At this time I saw five of the natives about the poor man they had killed, and two of them were beating him about the head with stones in their hands.

We had no time to reflect, for, to my surprise, they filled their canoes with stones, and twelve men came off after us to renew the attack; which they did so effectually as nearly to disable us all. We were obliged to sustain the attack without being able to return it, except with such stones as lodged in the boat. I adopted the expedient of throwing overboard some clothes, which, as I expected, they stopped to pick up; and as it was by this time almost dark, they gave over the attack, and returned towards the shore, leaving us to reflect on our unhappy situation.

And so they turned to the open sea. The rations of bread and water were kept to a minimum, and only with the addition of sea birds caught along the way were the men able to fare reasonably well. On May 28 they sighted the northeastern coast of Australia and on the following day the group landed. After 'a hot meal, the first in over a month, the condition and spirit of the crew seemed much improved, and they set sail the following day again.

On June 12 they sighted Timor, after having run by the log 3618 miles—undoubtedly one of the most extraordinary open boat voyages in history. Bligh wrote:

An indifferent spectator would have been at a loss at which most to admire, the eyes of famine sparkling at immediate relief, or the horror of their preservers at the sight of so many spectres, whose ghastly countenances, if the cause had been unknown, would rather have excited terror than pity. Our bodies were nothing but skin and bones, our limbs were full of sores, and we were clothed in rags. In this condition, with the tears of joy and gratitude flowing down our cheeks, the people of Timor beheld us with a mixture of horror, surprise and pity.

For two months the crew rested there, allowing Bligh to make a full report to the Admiralty. He was then able to obtain a ship, which he called the *Resource,* and set sail for Batavia on his way back to the homeland. Of the eighteen men who left the *Bounty* with Bligh, only eleven survived; the others died along the way.

Once back in England, Bligh became a national hero. At his court-martial for loss of the *Bounty* he was quite naturally acquitted.

In the meantime another ship, the *Pandora,* under the command of Captain Edwards, was dispatched to search for the *Bounty.* She was to proceed first to Tahiti and then to the other neighboring islands in an attempt to bring back as many of the mutineers as possible.

During this time, Captain Fletcher Christian of the *Bounty* and his crew of mutineers headed for Tupuai, an island about three hundred miles south of Tahiti, where they hoped to establish a colony. But they soon realized that they would first have to procure provisions and women from Tahiti itself. They arrived in Matavai Bay in June and answered the natives' questions about Bligh and the other men by saying that he had joined with Captain Cook on another island. The natives willingly supplied Christian with all he asked for and were delighted to learn that he intended to settle nearby. Once at Tupuai, Christian set about building a fort. However, because of disputes with the natives, the seamen decided to return to Tahiti.

Christian had one last request: "Gentlemen, I will carry you and land you wherever you please: I desire no one to stay with me, but I have one favour to request, that you will grant me the ship, tie the foresail, and give me a few gallons of water and leave me to run before the wind and I shall land upon the first island the ship drives to. I have done such an act that I cannot stay at Otaheite. I will never live where I may be carried home to be a disgrace to my family." Sixteen men returned to Tahiti and eight followed Christian. On September 21, 1789, the *Bounty* sailed once more with seven native men, twelve native women, and the nine mutineers—destination unknown. Some of the men remaining on Tahiti constructed a vessel in which they hoped to sail for the Dutch West Indies. Others wished to return to England. Disputes arose during this time in which two men were murdered.

On March 23, 1791, the *Pandora* arrived at Tahiti. The captain had those ex-members of the *Bounty* taken prisoners and clapped in irons. In May 1791 the *Pandora* embarked with the mutineers in search of the others, but after three futile months she came to disaster near the coast of Australia; she sailed into the Barrier Reef and sank rapidly, taking with her seven of the *Bounty* crew. The rest of the men were returned to England and were brought to trial.

At the trial of the ten accused, four men were acquitted, three condemned and executed, two condemned and pardoned, and one condemned and discharged on a point of law. During the trial Bligh lost some of the favor he had enjoyed and in time the interest in the *Bounty* disappeared. Nothing was heard of the ship, and it was assumed that she had been lost or that Christian and his men had been killed by the natives.

There are many contradictory stories. Actually, Christian and the few that were with him had sailed on to Pitcairn. To make sure that their whereabouts would not be discovered and to eliminate the temptation to leave, the crew burned the HMS *Bounty*.

What next occurred can only be surmised. We know that bloody feuds arose among the new islanders so that by 1800 only one of the original crew—Adams—was still alive. The others? That is a mystery still being unraveled and retold today.

For example, C. S. Wilkinson in *In the Wake of the Bounty* sets forth the intriguing claim that Christian grew bored after a couple of years and returned to England on one of the whaling ships that passed by Pitcairn. There are some data to substantiate this hypothesis, such as the fact that, while all the other mutineers had marked graves, there was none found for Christian. Why would they not clearly mark the grave of their leader, the man whom they had followed so faithfully to the end of the earth? Also, the sole survivor, the enigmatic Adams, gave various versions of how Fletcher died, once saying he had committed suicide and later claiming that the natives had killed him. Heywood, one of the pardoned mutineers back in England, claimed to have seen Fletcher in Plymouth around 1809. Wilkinson also is convinced that Coleridge became interested in the *Bounty* story, met Christian in England, and wrote the "Rime of the Ancient Mariner" around him!

In 1814 the warship *Briton* stopped at Pitcairn. By this time the colony had grown to forty-six and by 1823, when the *Comet,* an English vessel, arrived with orders to transport the colony to Tahiti, it had grown to eighty-seven members. They arrived at Papeete March 24 and were given land at Papaoa by Queen Pomare. However, the conditions were such that the people had only one desire—to return to their own island. This they did in time, but only after their number had been decimated by disease. To this day, approximately 125 of the descendants of these early mutineers and native colonists still survive on the two-mile area of Pitcairn.

Thus ended the romance of the *Bounty* and with it an era of color and excitement of Tahitian history ended in the minds of men. Henceforth the course of "Paradise" would seem to the world to be almost as materialistic and political as any other culture.

Until 1793 each island in the archipelago had its own government. The society was divided into three classes: the *ari'i-i'i* or petty kings and queens who made up the royal family, the *ra'atira* or small chiefs and landowners, and the *manahune* or common people. In this partially aristocratic organization, those of noble birth were believed to be descendants of the highest class of gods and were considered gods incarnate. This group owned the greater part of the land and had a large retinue of servants.

After the last departure of Captain Cook in 1777, a rather precarious peace was maintained on the island among the chiefs of the Tahitian districts. Chief Tuteha finally attacked Chief Vehiatua. Tuteha was killed and Hapai, ruler of the northern districts and father of Tu—who was to become the famous Pomare I—was among the defeated. Vehiatua's limited ambition allowed peace to be re-established. A short time later Vehiatua died and was succeeded by his son Vehiatua II. Pomare I, as has been mentioned, had begun to rule his own district about seven years earlier. He was just one minor leader among the thirteen chiefs on the greater peninsula and the six on the smaller. Unlike Vehiatua I, he was very ambitious, a fact which Cook made mention of on several occasions.

Although Tuteha was dead, his people continued to resent the presence of strangers in their midst. Their arrogance developed to such a point that Pomare I decided to take things into his own hands. His first move was to take over the district. This was the beginning of a whole series of island wars from which the Pomare leaders nearly always managed to emerge victorious.

In 1790 there was a revolution on Mooréa (Eimeo, as it was then called) in which the nephew of Pomare I was chased from the island. He later managed to reclaim his position, thanks to the help of his uncle, who had arms to aid him—those left by Captain Bligh's men.

When the war was quelled on Mooréa it arose again on Tahiti in several districts near the lands being used by survivors of the *Bounty*. The mutineers took a dim view of the war, but gave their support to Pomare, and he soon was the victor.

In 1791 Pomare II was made king of Tahiti, but his father continued to regulate the affairs of the country. The older man's desires for a kingdom had not abated, and he now had his eyes on the Leeward Islands (poetically called the "Islands under the Wind") which were more or less independent since the death of their king. To capture them he employed the aid of the sailors of the *Bounty,* and the Englishmen continued to aid him until they were captured by the *Pandora.* By the end of 1791, Pomare I had under his control all of Tahiti, Mooréa, and the island of Huahine. For the first time he seemed satisfied with his empire.

The other rulers of the districts appeared to accept the superior power of the Pomares. Even the Vehiatua family, who had adopted seamen Churchill and Thompson after their escape from the *Bounty,* also submitted to Pomare rule. Vehiatua III took Churchill as his "son" and at his request the Englishman at his death became Vehiatua IV. His brief career was spectacular, but was truncated when he was murdered out of jealousy by Thompson. Thompson in turn was killed by the followers of the chief. Their being no direct descendants in the Vehiatua line, the son of Chief Vaiuru became Vehiatua V.

Now begins a new phase in Tahitian history; many people consider it a disastrous one: the coming of the white settlers. There are stories of seamen who from time to time had made brief visits of several years, but there is no agreement among scholars about the identity of the first white settlers. It is only with the advent of the missionaries that we have certain knowledge of white men settling and remaining for extended periods of time in the Pacific Islands.

In 1795, the London Missionary Society, at the instigation of a Doctor Haweis, chaplain of Countess Huntington and co-founder of the society, decided to send missionaries to numerous islands in the Pacific. The doctor felt that there wouldn't be much trouble converting the natives and was so convincing in his arguments that he was able to obtain ten thousand pounds from public subscription. The English were anxious to acquire new territory, although ostensibly the government did little but facilitate the voyage—a privilege granted to all explorers.

In the eyes of the missionaries the "savage" nations were in a complete state of degradation and almost beyond redemption. The natives could no more grasp the concepts of one God or the Holy Savior than the missionaries could understand infanticide or tattooing.

The London Missionary Society obtained the ship *Duff* under the command of Captain Wilson, according to whom the object of the voyage was to deliver a portion of humanity from misery. Aboard the ship that left for Oceania were thirty missionaries and their families, each possessing—aside from their religious interests—some manual ability that would be advantageous in the new land.

In March 1797 the missionaries arrived at Matavai Bay and asked the king for land on which to establish their residences.

At first the missionaries found a rapport with Pomare I, who was still governing for his son, now seventeen years old. When the *Duff* departed on April 4, 1797, Pomare had already made himself special protector of the missionaries. One of the first and most necessary projects they undertook was learning the Tahitian language. Because English orthography was insufficient to transpose the Tahitian language, many of the linguistic inaccuracies of today can be attributed to those first attempts.

But the island's harmony soon became discord as rumors of war filled the air. The missionaries were expected to aid the chiefs in battle, as had the members of the *Bounty* in an earlier time; in addition, the constant pillaging compelled the missionaries to keep guard over their possessions night and day. Finally they called a meeting in which it was agreed that under no conditions would they take arms except to protect themselves from bodily harm.

An event which was to turn the islanders against the European settlers was precipitated shortly after the arrival at Matavai of the *Nautilus* under the command of Captain Bishop on March 6, 1798. Several seamen, having pilfered possessions from the missionaries, attempted to desert the ship and were apprehended. Pomare II, angry with all white men, on the advice of his chiefs decided to deny power to the protectors of the missionaries—his brother and his father, Pomare I. His objections were so strong that when the *Nautilus* took leave of Tahiti on March 30, 1798, eleven of the missionaries were on board. The remaining missionaries were left completely unprotected and at the mercy of the islanders; all their weapons were aboard the ship with the exception of two muskets given by them to Pomare I and his wife Idia.

It was other white settlers, however, who indirectly hampered the activities and safety of the missionaries. According to Ellis's journal, the influence of unprincipled white foreigners was more harmful for the missionaries and more detrimental to Christian influence than were the popular prejudices in favor of idolatry and the attachment of the priests to their gods.

Rumors of war persisted. The missionaries, asked to aid Pomare I in the coming struggle, replied that arms were made to defend, not to attack. However, Pomare I enlisted the aid of a native who had been taught to use a forge for tool-making and could make guns. When war came in 1798, Pomare I was prepared and victorious.

The land battles, according to Vincendon-Demoulin, nearly always had a definite pattern. It was a ludicrous concept of war, but probably no more so than any other concept of war. Once a plan of battle was established, the most celebrated warriors advanced, and when they drew near the enemy lines they all sat on the ground. Two or three among them then stood up and advanced a few steps, challenging their adversaries to fight; when the challenge was accepted there took place an exchange of terrifying threats. The men called out their own names and the names of their ancestors, recounting the prowess and exploits of their families, extolling the strength of their arms, and boasting of the glory that they were going to add to their names by the blows they were going to strike. They encouraged the enemy to come toward them so that their bodies could be offered to the gods for sacrifice. This exchange terminated and the battle began—a battle that often took place while the other men looked on as spectators.

Although the Tahitians had bows and arrows, they strangely did not use

them in war—perhaps under the charming theory that if they did someone might get hurt.

The battle began when at a certain distance the enemies opened
their ranks in order to let the sling throwers hurl their projectiles; the
skill of these men was dreaded and their reputation was great. Their
advance into battle was filled with piercing war cries. In actual hand-to-
hand combat they showed little skill, for in trying to hit the enemy on
the head with their stone weapons they relied more on their gods than
on their ability. When the first man fell, there was a great cry of triumph which was meant to fill the enemy with terror. The first victim
of the war was used for sacrifice. If a distinguished chief or warrior
was killed, his troops were reassembled at some distance to attack again.

Some battles were more for show than for anything else. Others were
more serious. Once a big one was over, as the missionary Ellis relates,
numerous atrocities were allegedly committed—among which was the
tipouta taata. This ghastly operation consisted of flattening out the body
with a club and then with a sharp stone cutting a large hole from the
stomach, through the back. The victorious warrior would put his head
through this hole and carry the victim bent in two—head in front, feet
in back, like a poncho—to the next battle. Sometimes human bones
were made into work tools or fish hooks.

When the war was over an offering was made to Oro, the god of war,
and the victors then divided the spoils and lands of their antagonists.
Then another victim was sacrificed to announce the end of hostilities
and the return to peace followed by a series of festivals.

The pattern of sea battles was also well defined. The combat took
place within the reefs, in the lagoon where the sea was always calm, the
pirogues or canoes arranged in one line, end to end. The objective of
this type of battle, known as *api*, was to prevent breaking the line or
fleeing during the battle. When the enemy had moved into a similar
position, the two fleets began to maneuver closer and closer to each
other with great cries. At a given distance, the warriors began throwing
stones with their slings and at shorter distances they used lances and

spearlike weapons. When they were side by side and hand to hand with the enemy, battle ensued. The lack of space, the impossibility of fleeing, made these sea fights savage encounters. It was a question of either winning or dying, and this made the men fight with a wild desperation.

Shortly after the defeat of Pomare II, various incidents occurred which alienated the Tahitians from the missionaries. Two English whalers appeared, and the natives thought that they had been sent to avenge their treatment of the missionaries. Greater difficulties arose when a present of gunpowder exploded while a chief was testing its quality, injuring several natives and the chief himself. When one of the missionaries went to the chief at Pomare I's request and applied medication, the chief's suffering increased, and he blamed the evil of the white man's medicine. A native doctor was then put in complete charge of the patient, and a short time later the chief died.

Pomare II was aided by such incidents in his quest for power. He took sides with the great priest Mani-Mani, whose influence on Mooréa and Tahiti was considerable, because of his knowledge of the "mysteries" and his ability to communicate with the gods.

Their combined forces attacked at Matavai while Pomare I was away from the area, sparing—strangely—the homes of the missionaries. Pomare II and Mani-Mani proclaimed that Pomare I was divested of all power and that his land was to be divided between themselves, his two captors. Pomare I thereupon sent his wife instructions to have Mani-Mani assassinated. Pomare II was unable to resist the repeated urgings of his mother, despite his close alliance to Mani-Mani. Ten days after the invasion of Matavai, on December 3, 1798, Mani-Mani was killed, and with his death the entire state of affairs on Tahiti was altered. Pomare and his son were reconciled and together they ameliorated temporarily the difficulties of the various districts.

In 1800 the construction of the first chapel on Tahiti was begun. This was the first positive step for the missionaries since their arrival on the island. On July 10, 1801, the *Royal Admiral* arrived with a new group of missionaries for the islands. Pomare, mainly to strengthen his political power on the island, gave them a warm welcome.

Gradually more and more ships began to stop at Tahiti on their way to Australia and other far points of the globe. When the *Norfolk* was shipwrecked, its crew established themselves on the island.

In the meantime, a rupture between the *ari'i-i'i* and the chief of Atehuru developed when the former expressed a desire to transport the idol Oro to Pare. Oro was said to be the son of Taaroa, god of creation, and was brought to Tahiti from the island of Raiatea. He was considered by many as the supreme god of the earth as well as the god of war. Pomare II claimed to have had a dream suggesting that the idol be moved from Atehuru to his own district. Not until he had this idol could the Pomares be the true and great rulers, for possession of Oro gave the owner certain political and religious privileges.

The maraes, such as the one in which Oro was enclosed, were open temples similar to an arena in the form of a parallelogram formed by a. stone wall six feet high and ending in an immense stone pyramid. The idol was placed in front of the pyramid. Each district or chief had at least one marae, within whose enclosure the priests of the district lived. Maraes were erected for all significant occasions, such as a great battle victory or the installation of an *ari'i-i'i*. The number of people participating was so great that if each man (women were not allowed in the marae) brought only one stone, a hundred-foot temple could be constructed.

The district chiefs along with the population of Atehuru formed the core of a many-factioned opposition to the Pomare rule. In their own opposition the chiefs were given considerable support from outcasts of other regions to whom they had granted asylum, from priests seeking vengeance for the death of Mani-Mani, and from the many islanders who considered the Pomares usurpers of the land.

Understandably, the Pomares, despite many efforts, could not convince the Atehuru chiefs to give up their Oro. Pomare I tried to subdue his son's impatience and anger at the refusal, but Pomare II organized a march to Atehuru. His seizure there of the idol began one of the longest wars ever to be waged on Tahiti, which was given the name *Te Tama'i a Rua*.

An event that was to have dire consequences in the battle for power was Pomare I's improper sacrifice of a servant. Every event of significance to the islanders—such as the ablutions of the royal offspring, the erection of a national marae, the launching of a large canoe—was an occasion for a human sacrifice. Most important during the time of war to assure protection and victory, a great number of sacrifices were made to Oro. Prior to a sacrifice it was the custom for the Chief to assemble the *ra'atira* in order to inform them that they must procure a sacrificial victim—a fact of which they were undoubtedly aware. The *ra'atira* could select a man only from among war captives (*titi*), men of the lowest rank (*manahune*), men of the middle classes who had made themselves obnoxious to those in power, blasphemers, and men who had escaped punishment for crimes. Once the victim was chosen, a member of the group clandestinely undertook the killing, at a time best calculated to keep the victim unaware of his fate (usually while he slept). The victim was hit carefully on the head with a stone, with great precautions taken against the possibility of disfiguring his face and making him unfit for offering. Servants then carried him to the temple in a basket among coconut leaves.

Victims were never chosen to satisfy a private quarrel, even if a chief desired it. If a chief insisted upon choosing a victim on a personal basis, he himself was designated to do the killing. However, in such cases it was customary for the *ra'atira* to be informed of the victim's identity, and they never failed to warn him of the impending danger. When no victim could be found—which was the usual case—and there was no one who had committed a grave enough crime, animals were used for sacrifice.

Yet the superiority of the human victim to the animal was certainly established. Morrison in his journal describes the sacrifice ritual of a human. He says that the priest removed the eyes from the victims with a piece of split bamboo

and placing them on a leaf, took a young plantain tree in one hand, and the eyes in the other. Then he made a long speech, holding them up to the young king, who sat above him with his mouth open; after he had ended his speech and laid the plantain trees before the young king, the bodies were removed and buried by his priests in the marae, and the eyes put up with the plantain trees on the altar.

I inquired the cause of the eye being offered, and was thus informed. The King is the Head of the people, for which reason the Head is sacred; the eye being the most valuable part is the fittest to be offered, and the reason the King sits with his mouth open, is to let the soul of the sacrifice enter into his soul, that he may be strengthened thereby, or that he may receive more strength of discernment from it, and they think that his tutelar deity or guardian angel presides to receive the soul of the sacrifice.

After such a prewar ceremony, the priest who acted as an oracle would tell the chief his possibilities of winning the proposed battle, usually conforming to the chief's desires in this matter.

And so, to propitiate Oro to win favor for the coming battle, Pomare sacrificed his own servant, disregarding the proper procedure of choosing sacrificial victims. In doing so he alienated many of his supporters.

For revenge, members of the Arahurahu district surrounded the district of Faaa, killed all the inhabitants, and burned their dwellings. Three hundred warriors from Mooréa came to help Pomare, but still the insurgents were able to push Pomare and his army back to Matavai, stopping there only because of the presence of Captain Bishop and his crew. However, the Arahurahu district threatened to return to attack and pillage the missionaries. Thanks to the presence of the crew from the *Norfolk* and the *Venus,* the men were able to band together for their protection. Knowing that the forces of Matavai were great, the enemy sent a messenger with propositions for an alliance.

While Pomare was in Tautira appeasing Oro, the enemy under great secrecy united for an all-out attack. Even though Pomare had heavier arms (forty muskets to fourteen), he was defeated, and as his troops fled to the hills they left the idol behind. Pomare and his forces moved back to Matavai, where Captain Bishop received them with open arms. Pomare and his son had only one thought—to flee into exile—but the missionaries persuaded them otherwise, and when the two saw the defenses the missionaries had established, they were encouraged. In addition, Captain Bishop told Pomare he would help him reconquer the power that was rightfully his. They went about fortifying their residences, and in fact demolished the chapel that Pomare had helped them to build so that the enemy could not set fire to it and thus jeopardize their homes. Daily they awaited attack from the enemy, who was in control of the greater part of the island. One day they received word that the peninsular half of the island was being attacked, which meant that Arahurahu was virtually without defenses. Moving into the area at night, Pomare and his troops found only old people, invalids, women, and children occupying the villages. By torchlight they massacred all of them. As Vincendon-Demoulin described it:

Two hundred cadavers scattered the road after Pomare's soldiers, evidence of their implacable cruelty. The horror of this atrocious butchery, committed without distinction of age or sex, not only fell back on Pomare who had ordered it and who found perhaps his excuse in the moeurs of the country, but must also be ascribed to a European, Andrew Lind, the Swede, who presided over this bloody work.

This vicious act caused the insurgents to vow destruction on the entire Pomare family. But Pomare, to reinforce his position, attacked first with the aid of the English. And again he barbarously killed all the prisoners.

Although the loss of life may not have been great in any of these battles, the ruin of plantations had a serious affect on the population, which was constantly decreasing.

Meanwhile, the missionaries attempted to continue their work. When peace was restored the chapel was rebuilt and the fields recultivated, but, great as was the effort the missionaries made, they were unable to make much headway with the natives. If there was hunger or an epidemic, it was impossible for a man to pray to a strange deity; it was more logical that the blame for every misfortune should be placed on the intruding strangers. And by failing to understand the native ways—one missionary, for example, felled the village breadfruit and coconut trees because he felt that the bountiful food supply so close at hand would contribute to idleness—the missionaries themselves were subverting their own work.

Pomare and his son both looked for a means to acquire new force and power. They sought arms from any strangers who stopped by the island. The elder never abandoned his plans regarding the complete possession of Arahurahu, and was preparing to attack the district when the *Margaret* anchored at Tahiti. Pomare greeted the crew enthusiastically and gave them every pleasure possible. Several days later he demanded gifts, the greatest being aid from the sailors in the war he was about to undertake. He made every effort to show them the justice of his enterprise, and when this had no effect he offered them the opportunity to pillage the district after its capture. He promised them meat, riches, and women. The sailors of the *Margaret* could not refuse this last offer, and finally agreed to accompany Pomare. Their captain's opposition to the project was useless.

After the sacrifice to propitiate the gods and bring protection to the soldiers, Pomare I and Pomare II joined together with ten Europeans and the district soldiers to attack. They advanced slowly and cautiously. Ellis, the missionary, in discussing this particular effort, stated that in the summer of 1803 a large group of chiefs and soldiers were reunited in Arahurahu and that when Pomare II demanded the idol Oro again it was simply handed to him without resistance. However, Turnbull relates that, although the chiefs would have resisted Pomare, they were aware of being outnumbered by a superior force and were therefore without any choice other than submission.

This simple victory was to be enjoyed by Pomare I for only a short period, for, suddenly in 1803, the Napoleon of Tahiti died. The circumstances surrounding his death are unclear. It was blamed on the missionaries by some, on his sacrilege against Oro by others.

It is interesting to note that Pomare I was known under a different name to nearly every notable European who ventured to Tahiti in early times. To Cook he was Otou; to Bligh, Tina; he also referred to himself as Vaaratoa; finally he took the name Pomare. The origin of the name, which literally means night cough (po—night, mare—cough) is said to have come during an excursion made in the mountains. During the night he was forced to stop, became cold, and took sick. Toward morning he began coughing endlessly. His servants in speaking of that night referred to it as the "pomare." The sound of the word so appealed to the chief that he adopted it as his own.

Of all who regretted Pomare's death, perhaps the missionaries had the greatest cause to do so. But despite all his help to them, it has been suggested that Pomare never really understood the missionaries' intentions. He understood that they were "priests" and, as was the case with the Tahitian priests, he considered them invaluable to war, which was inevitable in his struggle for power. He also expected them to add their support to the war effort, since they had come on ships, as had the men of the *Bounty* who had helped him fight earlier. It did not take him long to realize that these strangers came not to help with war but to deter it.

However, Pomare and his people were eager to learn all they could from the clerics about molding iron, though this advantage was small when compared to all that the natives disliked about the missionaries. The white man had brought new diseases to Tahiti, and he was easy to blame for the epidemics and strange deaths that occurred.

Discontent among the islanders and between them and the missionaries mounted until it appeared that there would be open revolts. Young and inexperienced in actual political practices, Pomare II found himself without any guidance. He was able to maintain a precarious peace, however, from 1804 to 1806, during which time the missionaries tried to continue their work. By the time that fire destroyed their own crops, their position had become so bad that they dared not ask for anything. Their aid from Europe was drastically cut and the situation became so unbearable that in 1806 several missionaries left Tahiti.

As more of his early supporters defected to the enemy, Pomare's position declined, and when he began out-and-out hostility in attacking the insurgents he was (despite a prediction of victory) decisively beaten, losing most of his arms together with a great part of his army. He fled to Pare and shortly afterward sought asylum on Mooréa. The remaining missionaries, frightened by the pillaging and destruction of the victors, fled to neighboring islands.

Tati was then called to lead the new government, and the victors undertook to make reprisals on the English. The missionaries discovered such intentions, but not in time to stop the *Venus* from anchoring. The ship was captured, her second mate murdered, her crew thrown overboard, and those that were spared were to be offered to Oro in sacrifice. Fortunately the *Hibernia* arrived in time to aid some of the survivors.

Pomare II, in the interim, had called on the chiefs of the other islands of the archipelago and attempted, with their backing, to retake Tahiti. Again he was defeated.

Pomare continued to live in exile on Mooréa, and there he first began to abandon his own religious beliefs with the sincere desire to take those of the white man. His own gods had failed him and he sought new ones; moreover, he hoped in doing so to regain the support of the English. The exiled king once more pursued his lessons in reading and writing and became the first of a small group of natives the missionaries were able to convert.

On the island of Tahiti during this time disorder and anarchy reigned. Again there was talk of war, and now rumors of a possible invasion of Mooréa. Two Tahitian chiefs came to Pomare just at the time when he was to embrace Christianity and persuaded him once again to take over the government on the main island. On August 13, 1812, he returned home.

During his stay on Mooréa Pomare II had indulged in whisky as well as in religion, and the latter did little to temper his drunkenness. It has been said that during his drunken periods he lost all restraint and was quick to kill his subjects at the least provocation. He demanded liquor from all the ships that stopped and was brought rum by visiting whalers. Liquor was given only to the district chiefs, but soon the people demanded similar treatment and the rum brought to the island was insufficient. The natives, following the instructions of the Europeans, began to distill their own drink from the root of the *ti* plant. The first and strongest yield, called *ao*, was given to the chiefs and the second was shared among the remainder of the population. Drunkenness among the natives increased to such an extent that it once more became dangerous for ships to anchor.

But much of what the natives did can be attributed directly to plain vengeance. The conduct of many of the foreign sailors on the islands was far from exemplary, and the little good they did was overshadowed by their interference in island life. The situation was so severe, in fact, that in 1813 the government of New South Wales (Australia) issued a proclamation stating that any crimes committed on the islands by sailors would automatically subject them to a fine of one thousand pounds. They were to take no sides in native quarrels, take no part in island wars, do nothing to hinder native religious celebrations, and take no women without the consent of both the family and the individual; the natives, the proclamation declared, were under the protection of His Majesty, and all acts of pillage, rape, piracy, murder, and other such attempts on people and property would be severely punished.

Even with the antagonism toward the white men, the number of Christian sympathizers among the natives had grown considerably by 1814 until the number regularly partaking of services reached about three hundred. The missionary schools were attended by a growing number of students, and religious services were organized on nearly all the islands of the archipelago by both the missionaries and the converts. Pomare himself, in an attempt to persuade the large portion of natives who seemed to sway between the doctrines of Christianity and those of Oro, told them to burn their idols and embrace the one real God.

The number of Christians continued to grow, and those who had escaped to Mooréa had a great effect on the natives there. Curious about the new religion, anxious for peace, and influenced by Pomare, many more of the islanders began to mix with the Christians and soon began taking instruction from the missionaries. The missionary records indicate that by 1815 school attendance had reached almost six hundred and fifty on Mooréa, and there was an insufficient number of books available. On Tahiti, Christianity was spread by the remaining Christians to the extent that by the middle of 1815 the number of Christians there almost equaled the number of pagans.

With the return of all the missionaries to the island, the old Tahitian way of life was changed forever. Their emphasis on Christian doctrine soon led to their desire to institutionalize Christian or European laws as well—laws poorly suited to the culture of a Pacific island. By 1816, when nearly the entire archipelago was converted, the missionaries ceased to direct their work toward merely religious ends and began actually to administrate the islands according to their own laws.

What replaced ancient rules governing family, class, and society in general was not easily adaptable to the population. Perhaps a basic difficulty in their adjustment stemmed from the fact that they had heretofore considered the chiefs as god figures to whom they could turn in need, and now they had only one invisible God. Obviously, what was needed was a set of rules adaptable to a modern Tahitian society; but the native Tahitian leaders were unable to construct such a constitution and they had turned to the missionaries for aid. Unfortunately these "religious leaders" had learned nothing from their earlier attempts to impose unrealistically strict laws on the natives, and they again outlawed such ancient pleasures as dancing, forbade tattooing, and fire-and-brimstoned about the sinfulness of not observing the Sabbath.

Pomare continued to rule as the "Christian King," but his apparent fervor for religion was contradicted by the actual manner in which he led his life. He had two wives—Terimiomio and Ariipaia—and he continued to drink heavily. As he grew older he was seldom seen sober, and it was said that he always carried a Bible under one arm and a bottle of rum under the other. This hobby took its toll, and toward the end of 1821 he fell ill and died.

The loss of this man to the archipelago was of such great consequence that at his death there arose a threat of reversion to the ancient ways. His son was then only a year old, and the people found themselves without a ruler. The missionaries, seeking to protect the place of the Church by eventually heading the state with a Christian-educated Pomare III, objected to the suggestion that Tati become sovereign and, instead, enabled Teremiomio to become regent and Pomare Vahine Ariipaia, Pomare's second wife, to succeed her in an equally unsuccessful and unpopular rule. Aimata, Pomare II's daughter, married a young chief of Tara a year after her father's death and settled on Tahiti. (Marriages generally took place when the parties were between the ages of twelve and sixteen, and unions could be broken easily.) At this time she had no intention of ruling the island, for her brother had already been named successor to the throne.

With the death of Pomare II and with their influence over the regent, the English, after a long struggle for the domination of the island, were now virtually in control. The lower classes showed their discontent with this control by abandoning the church, and disorder was again brought to the island.

As though in protest against the English rule, the forbidden practice of tattooing came back into vogue. It was done with a liquid extracted from the burnt seed of the *tiairi* fruit. Girls were tattooed for beauty usually at the age of about eight or ten, only on the hands, calves, feet, thighs, and hips. Tattooing always began on the hips, and not until it was done were the girls allowed to wear clothes. Up to that time they went about naked.

In 1824 the coronation of the child Pomare III took place amid sober Christian splendor very different from the animated installations of previous Tahitian kings. Shortly after, he was sent to Mooréa and put in the hands of Reverend Orsmond, director of a special school for children of missionaries and exceptionally bright native students.

Reports of the English missionary establishments were at the time floating back into France and getting much public attention. The press was attacking the English efforts in Tahiti, and *Le Drapeau Blanc* openly criticized the Protestant missions and voiced doubts about the English puritans. The political climate in France at this time made every question significant, and Tahiti thus took on an unaccustomed importance. Also, nineteenth-century romanticism made the "noble savage" on a Pacific isle seem very attractive.

The first Tahitian government quarrel with the European powers erupted in 1825 when Pomare Vahine Ariipaia, aware of the value the Europeans placed on mother-of-pearl, temporarily imposed taxes on the oysters to augment Tahitian revenues.

The missionaries began to make efforts to industrialize the island and to develop it agriculturally. Crops of sugar and tobacco were cultivated; the natives were taught iron-working and carpentry. But by 1826 the original burst of energy had subsided and the population was once more returning to its old ways. Living on Tahiti was a nonchalant affair; one worked only for what was necessary for daily living. Perhaps this attitude over the years has done more to discourage missionary efforts than anything else.

The missionaries were at first successful in their attempts to develop the manufacture of cotton cloth, but soon the novelty of this disappeared. The attitude was: "Why should we work? Haven't we enough breadfruits, coconuts and bananas to nourish us? It is good for the Europeans to work; they have to have beautiful clothes and beautiful ships. We are content with what we have."

With such efforts at industrialization and agricultural development came the introduction of silver money to Tahiti and a new concept of trading. What the natives attempted to buy was out of proportion to the real value of the objects in question; they ignored the value of silver and were willing to exchange it for worthless objects on which they placed great value. Though the Tahitians liked some European products and wanted them, they soon had nothing to offer in exchange.

Trade got so out of hand that at one point most of the rights of the inhabitants of the island had been given over in exchange for imported materials. The number of ships that stopped at Tahiti continued to increase; whalers came for supplies, and traders, adventurers, and explorers dropped anchor there. As the state of the Tahitians continued to deteriorate, the missionaries placed increasing blame on the sailors. New laws were constructed to deal with the relationships between foreign vessels.

Toward the end of the year Pomare III became ill with a malady that was ravaging the population, and in 1827 he died. So at the age of sixteen Aimata was made ruler of Tahiti. The missionaries had put all their efforts into her brother and now they were faced with a girl-queen whose education had been almost completely neglected.

With Aimata's rise to power the Tahitians further resisted the strict codes imposed by the missionaries and returned once more to old native practices. Dancing again became a popular pastime, and native songs were sung instead of the Christian hymns.

At this time, a strange cult began to develop on the island despite efforts of both natives and missionaries to subdue it. The members grew so fast that they soon threatened to dominate the island. The sect, called the Mamaia, originated with Teaou, deacon of the church at Puna-auia.

The Mamaia was apparently the outgrowth of a combination of native religion and Christianity. Its members believed in Jesus Christ, read the Bible, and prayed, but these were the only restrictions placed on them; they were otherwise free to act according to their desires. The example for marriage was taken from Solomon, who they knew was wise, and they felt that if he could have several wives they could too. They did not believe in hell and felt that everyone would go to heaven. Pleasure for everyone was the essential. It is not surprising that the sect succeeded supremely well.

Early in 1829, Jacques Moerenhout, one of the best chroniclers of Tahiti, arrived, hoping to develop the island's trade. He wrote that the commerce situation had reached a new low. Aimata had begun to take power into her own hands and to drink heavily, as her father had. She pursued pleasure relentlessly, surrounded herself with other merry-makers, and soon gave up most of her acquired and detested European ways.

After Aimata made a brief trip to her husband's home, she returned to Tahiti to find talk of war—for the first time in nearly fifteen years. The dissension grew between the Mamaia, which had now begun to show its political power, and several opposing chiefs. Class divisions became sharper, the ruling family, the chiefs, and the populace having little to do with each other.

During this time of dissension, new interests had started to enter Tahiti. The first Roman Catholic missionaries had already established themselves on the Gambier Islands in 1834 with hopes of taking their place on Tahiti as well. Their coming brought with it even more of the complexities of the "civilized" world.

As early as 1774 two Catholic missionaries had tried to set up a mission on Tahiti with no success. But now in May 1835 the Irish catechist Colomban Murphy en route to the Sandwich Islands stopped at Tahiti and had an interview with the Queen, much to the dismay of George Pritchard, an active Protestant missionary, British Consul, merchant, and sinister figure in this part of Tahiti's history. Murphy found several chiefs sympathetic to his ideas, even if Pritchard was not, and conveyed this idea to the French.

On November 20, 1836, two French Catholic missionaries, Fathers Laval and Caret, arrived at Tahiti. Their arrival had been anticipated by Pritchard, who called a meeting of most of the chiefs. He had persuaded them to guard the coast and prevent the arrival of the *Elisa*, but the ship somehow anchored successfully and the priests immediately visited Jacques Moerenhout, who had recently been appointed consul for the United States. At Papeete the clerics were received by Queen Pomare with Pritchard standing by her elbow. Moerenhout and Pritchard had always been friendly, but the latter's refusal to accept the newcomers caused an immediate break and Moerenhout continued to help the Catholics from then on. Pritchard had a strange hold over the Queen, and through her he threatened to use force if the Catholics did not leave. Finally the priests were forced to barricade themselves in a house, desperately hoping that opinion against them would change. A short time later, several men dragged the priests from the house and placed them forcibly aboard an English schooner.

The question of Catholicism for the first time raised a new political problem for the islands—that of outside interests. Until this time the English had been the sole and dominating force. However, Catholicism and France were as one, and as a result two maritime world powers were indirectly brought face to face.

It is understandable that the English did not want another faction to seize the rewards of their labors. But a large portion of the difficulties that arose must be blamed on George Pritchard, who was the English strong arm.

When the Catholic missionaries arrived back in France word had already reached the government about their treatment, and the French took it as a direct offense. They deemed it necessary to intervene for the protection of French nationals. Word was sent to Abel Dupetit-Thouars, commander of the *Venus,* then at Valparaiso, to proceed to Tahiti to investigate the charges and ask damages from the Queen for the insults made to the French priests.

In the interval between the departure of the French missionaries and the arrival of Dupetit-Thouars, a feeling of unrest existed among the Tahitians; they were awaiting some sort of retaliation that they knew would come. Moerenhout maintained his position with the Catholics and soon found himself head of a group, first political and then Catholic, and finally French. In the beginning of 1838 an attempt was made on the life of Moerenhout by two men who were supposedly foreigners. When he was attacked, Moerenhout cried out and his wife ran to his aid. He was severely wounded and his wife was beaten so savagely that she died soon afterward.

Dupetit-Thouars arrived on the *Venus* in August of the same year and went immediately to Moerenhout, who confirmed the accusations of the French government. The next day Dupetit-Thouars went to the Queen, demanded damages, and declared that if the wishes of France were not complied with within twenty-four hours his country could be considered in a state of hostility with Tahiti. Pritchard, representing the Queen, went to Dupetit-Thouars. The Tahitian government, he said, was naturally in no position to oppose a major force, but the Queen would agree only to part of the demands. A compromise was made and a letter of apology sent to King Louis Philippe.

By September, there was harmony between the French and the Tahitians. Dupetit-Thouars and the Queen made an agreement that any Frenchman would be welcomed and protected by the Tahitians, as would any Tahitian who visited France. Moerenhout was subsequently appointed French Consul.

But Pritchard's power was steadily increasing as he carried on more and more trade with the natives. After the *Venus* departed he broke all agreements made with the French and saw to it that a law was passed prohibiting foreigners from purchasing land on Tahiti, thus eliminating the possibility of a French settlement. He also pushed through a law forbidding "doctrines contrary to those in effect" from being taught. Under Pritchard's influence, Queen Pomare wrote to Queen Victoria telling her that her nationality and her faith were the two things closest to her heart and that she needed the help of England to protect these things, primarily from the French. Queen Victoria answered that she hardly knew the French, but thought that they should be welcomed to Tahiti.

In 1839 the French frigate *Artémise,* under the command of Captain

Laplace, set sail from Sydney. In trying to anchor at Tahiti, the ship hit a reef and the Queen refused to aid the French crew. When Laplace was finally rescued he wangled a meeting with Queen Pomare and managed to make a great impression upon her. Such was his charm that in spite of Pritchard the Queen issued a statement granting Catholicism free rein on Tahiti and on any of Pomare's other possessions. French Catholics were to be accorded all the privileges given to the Protestant missionaries. Laplace also negotiated land for a Catholic mission.

Relations between the French and Tahitians were cemented once and for all when the French *Pylade* anchored at Tahiti in July 1840, and the Queen came aboard. This further alarmed Pritchard, who had used every means he knew to turn the Tahitians against the French. He immediately left for England with hopes of securing aid from Queen Victoria. But he arrived in the midst of a parliamentary upheaval, and the Tahitian question was shoved aside.

The Tahitians were gradually becoming aware that they were now dealing not only with religions but with nations, and that the Catholics and Protestants on the islands were trying to utilize the power of their mother countries. Although Queen Pomare attempted to be friendly with both the French and the English, this feeling was not shared by the populace as a whole. French whalers, for example, often complained of the treatment given them by Tahitian "police."

Shortly after the departure of the *Pylade*, Father Caret returned to Tahiti and was more or less peacefully tolerated until he tried to build a chapel. Then the situation became so serious that he was once again driven from the island. This off-again-on-again attitude toward the Catholics shows how chaotic conditions were at this time.

Although Queen Pomare was ostensibly in control, the district chiefs were sharply divided into two religious camps. They all seemed aware that Tahiti could not continue to exist without the aid of a foreign country—but which one? Those who favored the French were the most influential; also, since no response had come from England after they had requested protection, there was no choice but to turn to France.

View of Papeete harbor showing Queen Pomare's house.

Already Nuku-Hiva, in the Marquesas, had been made a protectorate of France under the guidance of Dupetit-Thouars; this allowed the French greater efficiency in operating in the Pacific.

Dupetit-Thouars stopped at Tahiti again in August 1842 and found that the state of the Catholic missionaries had not noticeably improved, that those who were to have been punished for misdeeds against the French were free. He wrote Queen Pomare demanding that ten thousand piasters be deposited with his government as a precaution against further injustice to his compatriots; otherwise, force would be used.

When the chiefs saw the demand they came to the conclusion that the time had come, since they could no longer govern themselves, to ask France for protection. The message was sent to Dupetit-Thouars, who immediately agreed, but had to first obtain approval from the King. Pritchard was not present and could exert no influence. Queen Pomare was on Mooréa preparing to give birth to her third child.

The statement received contained the following conditions: (1) That the sovereignty of the Queen and her authority and the authority of the chiefs over their people would be guaranteed. (2) That all the laws and rules would be made in the name of Queen Pomare and signed by her. (3) That the possession of lands belonging to the Queen and the people would remain with them; all disputes relative to the right of ownership or owners of the land would be under a special jurisdiction of a tribunal of the land. (4) That everyone would be free to exercise his own religion. (5) That the churches already there would continue, the English missionaries would go about their duties without being bothered, and no one would be molested for his beliefs.

All the chiefs as well as Pomare signed this document. The same day, September 9, 1842, Dupetit-Thouars informally accepted the Queen's proposal, repeating in his letter the conditions stipulated by her. In addition an official communication was sent to all foreign governments concerned, asking for an end to all difficulties with the Tahitians, and including excerpts from the Queen's demands.

Dupetit-Thouars next proceeded to organize a provisionary council and await the ratification of his French government by Louis Philippe. This was done on March 25, 1843, and with it another new era began on the island.

In 1843 Pritchard returned to Tahiti on the *Vindictive* with Captain Toup Nicholas, a long-time foe of the French, intending to destroy the protectorate by force if necessary. Pritchard did not wait to disembark at Papeete, but landed at Papara and immediately began crusading among the natives against the French. The vacillating Queen was unable to take a stand, and once again she slipped under the influence of Pritchard. The chiefs, however, were not so easily swayed by the maneuvers of the English. Captain Nicholas was making every effort to strengthen Pritchard's position, but he did not openly violate the law and nothing could be done to stop him. He addressed a proclamation telling all English inhabitants of the island to ignore the French authority and conform only to the native rule. Pritchard, of course, had personal motives as well as a general dislike for the French. He had come from England to Sydney on a commerce ship which arrived at Papeete shortly after the *Vindictive* and included in its cargo copper money intended for Tahitian circulation. Since Pritchard was the principal merchant on the island, it would not have been long before all the silver money in circulation would have been in his hands in exchange for the coppers. The provisionary government did all it could to prevent the circulation of the money, but the Queen under Pritchard's influence authorized it. Fortunately, Pritchard's enemies ran through the villages warning the people that the copper coins were valueless.

Pritchard was not so easily dissuaded, and his next move was to tell the people from the pulpit of the church in Papeete that he had obtained the money from England, and that therefore it had to have value, that it was authorized by the Queen. This made some impression on them, but then a canny native tried to buy English goods from Pritchard himself with coppers instead of silver coins—and quite naturally was refused. Word of this spread like wildfire, and from that time on Pritchard's money was totally discredited.

But the merchant and the captain were not finished. Through their own efforts and their power over the Queen they caused a near reign of terror on the island. In fact, they were influential enough to make Pomare write Queen Victoria that she had been forced by fear to sign the agreement for protection under the French, and that she needed English help. Captain Nicholas's efforts were brought to a sudden halt, however, when he was instructed to leave Tahiti by a superior officer who was in command of the South Seas. Nicholas was smart enough to deny his efforts against the French rule before leaving, and instead asked that the people uphold the rules of the protectorate. Pritchard, after his ally had deserted him, was forced into recognizing the French provisionary government.

Dupetit-Thouars was in the Marquesas when he received official approval from the French King for the protectorate of Tahiti, and at the same time news of his nomination to the Legion of Honor. In addition he was informed that M. Bruat had been appointed governor of French establishments under his direction in Oceania. On November 1, 1843, he returned to Tahiti and immediately informed the Queen of the French acceptance.

The same day two ships, the *Uranie* and the *Danaë*, arrived, and on one of them was the new governor. But when the Queen refused to accept his flag, the French tricolor, difficulty immediately arose. Queen Pomare, once again under Pritchard's influence, would not even consult with Dupetit-Thouars. He was obliged to threaten that if the agreement of 1842 were not recognized he would be compelled to use force and remove the Queen from her position, taking possession of the island under the name of the King of France.

On November 6 troops were disembarked for this purpose. In November 1843 Dupetit-Thouars set sail for the Sandwich Islands, leaving Bruat in full command of Tahiti. Shortly thereafter, recognition of

RIGHT: *Louis Philippe I, King of France.*

BELOW: *Queen Victoria of England, to whom Queen Pomare wrote that her "nationality and her faith were . . . closest to her heart and that she needed the help of England to protect these things, primarily from the French."*

121

French occupation was made by the chiefs of all the islands of the archipelago.

Queen Pomare continued to side with the English Consul Pritchard, who was no longer recognized by the French because of his actions. They finally demanded that he be transferred to the Samoan Islands, at this time still inhabited by a rather primitive people and rarely visited by outsiders; Pritchard rejected this suggestion.

Even his projected removal did not insure peace on the island. The continued proximity of English ships caused unrest particularly to the Queen, who felt that the entire royal family was in danger. Along with several discontented chiefs, they moved to the smaller half of the island, formed a party hostile to the French, and attempted to rally more rivals. In the midst of this, a letter from Lord Aberdeen, Minister of Foreign Affairs, to Pritchard fell into the hands of the English missionary Orsmond, who had attempted to keep peace on the island. The letter declared that the English government would not intervene in French affairs. Unfortunately this letter was kept secret, and the result was a series of bloody encounters.

At first nothing but vague rumors were circulated. But in March 1844 it was stated that three thousand men were about to march and a state of siege was declared. The French took this opportunity to arrest Pritchard, although there was some doubt as to the effect it might have on Anglo-French relations. Pritchard was finally forced to leave Tahiti, but his report about French behavior was so strong that the English demanded an explanation from the French government. Louis Philippe, who wanted to avoid war, heard the arguments and believed it best to disclaim Dupetit-Thouars.

But the frigate *Charte* had already arrived from the Marquesas, bringing troops. Moerenhout, now a government member, left for Mooréa to raise the French flag there, and Bruat, with the aid of Orsmond, managed to gather all those to Tahiti who had fled in fear.

On March 21, 1844, the Tahitians began the first of a series of guerrilla attacks. With the aid of the natives, the French scored continual victories. But then the news arrived that Louis Philippe had discredited Dupetit-Thouars; this was a severe setback. Bruat felt compelled to return the title to Queen Pomare, and this action encouraged the rebels. The Queen, in a state of confusion, refused the title. In 1845, since no agreement could be made with her, Paraita was appointed regent by Bruat, who continued to govern the island without the help of the King.

In May of the same year, the district chiefs and judges convened to revise the now outdated laws that had been made in 1824 at the encouragement of the English missionaries. There were angry mutterings, and finally a large number of insurgents, estimated at about twelve hundred, attempted to attack Papeete. Though their attack was repulsed, they frightened a segment of the population into fleeing. Other lesser attacks followed, in which the French as well as the natives lost men.

With the submission of Papeete, peace was slowly restored in district after district and the "revolt" was finally ended by the beginning of 1847. The Queen, who was self-exiled, wanted to return when Bruat came back as governor. He agreed, and she put her entire family in the hands of the French and swore to cooperate fully with the protectorate government. The greatest prosperity that the island had ever known in modern times came to Tahiti.

Little by little the English missionaries departed. They left behind them, however, a significant mark on Tahitian culture: over fifty thousand pages printed in Tahitian, the Bible which had been printed in Tahitian in 1835, an Anglo-Tahitian dictionary printed in 1851, and, of course, a ruined paradise that would never be as beautiful as they had found it.

After their departure, the Legislative Assembly asked the Reformed Church of France to send French pastors; the first, Benjamin Arbousset, arrived in 1863 and proceeded to reopen the schools and organize the parishes. Since that time the Tahitian church has remained under the supervision of the Société des Missions Evangeliques de Paris.

Both Protestant and Catholic schools continued to function even under the French. In 1883 the government took all official education under its control.

Queen Pomare by now was an old woman who had seen great changes since the days when she was known as Aimata. In the end, she remained true to the French and followed Bruat's leadership loyally.

Pierre Loti, a French naval officer and author of the popular book *Rarahu,* describes her thus at this period:

The scene took place at Queen Pomare's palace in November, 1872.

The court, which commonly goes barefoot, lying on the fresh grass or on mats of pandanus fiber, was in full dress that evening, keeping high festival.

I was at the piano; before me was the score of the *Africaine.* This piano, which had only that morning arrived, was a novelty at the court of Tahiti; it was a costly instrument with a soft, rich tone, like the notes of an organ or of distant bells, and Meyerbeer's music was to be heard for the first time in the halls of Pomare. Standing by me was my shipmate Randle, who subsequently left the sea to become a leading tenor in the American opera houses; he enjoyed a brief spell of fame under the name of Randetti, until, having taken to drink, he died in abject poverty.

He was just now in full possession of his voice and gifts, and never have I heard a man's voice more touching or more exquisite. He and I together charmed many Tahitian ears, for in that land music is instinctively understood by all, even by the most savage natives.

At the upper end of the room, under a full-length portrait of herself—painted by a clever artist some thirty years before, and representing her as handsome and idealized—sat the old queen on her gilt throne, which was covered with red brocade. In her arms was her now dying grandchild, little Pomare V, who fixed her large black eyes, glittering with fever, on my face. The old woman's ungraceful bulk filled the whole breadth of her seat. She was dressed in a loose gown of crimson velvet; a stockingless ankle was laced in slipshod fashion into a satin boot. By the side of the throne was a tray full of pandanus cigarettes.

An interpreter in evening dress stood close at hand, for this woman, who understood French as well as any Parisian, never in her life would utter a single word of it.

The admiral, the governor, and the consuls had seats near Her Majesty.

There still was dignity in that face, brown, wrinkled, set and hard as it was; above all else it was sad, infinitely sad—with watching as death snatched from her all her children, one after another, all stricken with the same incurable malady; with seeing her kingdom invaded by civilization and fast breaking up, her lovely island degraded to a scene of debauchery.

The windows were open to the gardens, and outside heads could be seen crowned with flowers, and moving to and fro as they came closer to hear. All the women in attendance on the queen; Faimana, wreathed like a naiad with water plants and reeds; Tehamana with a crown of datura, Teria, Raourea, Tapou, Erere, Tairea, Tiahoui and Rarahu.

The side of the room opposite to where I sat was all open; there was no wall, only a colonnade of timber, and beyond it the Tahitian landscape under a star-sown sky.

At the feet of the columns, against that dark, remote background, rose a whole row of figures seated on a bench; the ladies of rank these, princesses or chiefs in their own right. Four gilt candelabra of Pompadour style, astonished at finding themselves amid such surroundings, lighted them fully and showed off their dresses, which were really very elegant and handsome. Their feet, naturally small, were neatly shod in irreproachable satin boots.

Here was the splendid Ariinoore, in a tunic of cherry-colored satin and a garland of peia—Ariinoore, who refused to marry Lieutenant M_____, of the French Navy, though he had ruined himself in buying her a corbeille,— and who had also rejected Kamehameha V, king of the Sandwich Islands.

By her side sat Paüra, her inseparable friend, a fascinating type of savage with her singular ugliness—or beauty? A head that would eat raw fish or human flesh—a strange creature, dwelling in the forest wilds of a remote district, with the education of an English Miss—waltzing, too, like a Spaniard.

Then Titaua, who charmed Prince Alfred of England, the only Tahitian who ever preserved any beauty in her riper years; she was a constellation of splendid pearls and crowned with fluttering *revareva*. Her two daughters, just come home from a school in London, were as handsome as their mother.

They wore European ball dresses, half-disguised, out of regard for the queen's prejudices, under Tahitian tapas of white gauze.

Princess Ariitea, Pomare's daughter-in-law, with her sweet, innocent, dreamy face, faithful to her own headdress of China roses caught here and there in her flowing hair.

The queen of Bora-Bora, a thorough old savage with pointed teeth, in a velvet dress.

Queen Moe (*moe* meaning sleep or mystery) in a dark robe; regular features and a mystical type of face, with strange eyes half-shut, and an expression of introspection, like some old-fashioned portraits.

Behind these groups, in broad candlelight, rose the mountain peaks, dark in the transparent atmosphere of the Oceanian night, sharply outlined against the starry sky; and in the foreground the picturesque mass of a clump of bananas with their enormous leaves and bunches of fruit, looking like colossal candelabra ending in great black flowers. As a background to these trees the nebulae of the southern hemisphere spread a sheet of blue light, and in the middle blazed the Southern Cross. Nothing could be more ideally tropical than this faraway perspective.

The air was full of that exquisite fragrance of orange blossom and gardenia which is distilled by night under the thick foliage; there was a great silence, accentuated by the bustle of insects in the grass, and that sonorous quality, peculiar to night in Tahiti, which predisposes the listener to feel the enchanting power of music.

The piece we chose was Vasco's song when he walks alone in the island he has just discovered, intoxicated with admiration for its strange new aspect —a passage in which the composer has perfectly represented all he knew by intuition of the remote glories of these lands of light and verdure. And Randle, with a glance at the scene around him, began in his lovely voice:

> "Land of wondrous beauty, gardens of delight
> O Paradise!—risen from the waters!"

The shade of Meyerbeer must have felt a thrill of pleasure that evening, at hearing his music thus rendered at the other side of the world.

On September 17, 1877, the Queen died and her body was buried at Papaoa with great ceremony. She left her thirty-nine-year-old son

Papeete, showing the bakery and government storehouse at the end of the last century. This view is from the site of the present naval base. The point of land with the coconut palms in the middle distance is the present site of Les Tropiques hotel.

This is the part of Papeete which has changed the
least since the turn of the century, when this photo
was taken. There are a few more yachts, a few more
people, and a lot more motor scooters.

Another view of the Papeete that Gauguin knew.
It has changed surprisingly little in over half a
century.

128

A naïve and charming wedding photo taken at about the same time as the pictures opposite.

Ariiane to hold the now ineffectual and rather pathetic title of King Pomare V. Shortly after, Ariiane married Marau Salmon and was crowned Pomare V. The governor, captain of the *Planche*, tried unsuccessfully to persuade him to unite Tahiti with France. But finally the King met with his chiefs and signed an agreement in June 1880, making a gift of Pomare's possessions to France.

For the past fifty years or so, Tahiti has remained much the same as it was at the turn of the century. Of course, there have been more tourists, more books have been written about the island, more scientific studies have been made, and more people have enjoyed themselves there as the fame of the island has spread. And as the education of the native population has increased, there has been an increasing need for more independent government. The French, therefore, have instituted a new administrative policy throughout French Polynesia. On July 26, 1957, the legal name of French Oceania was changed to French Polynesia and the law introduced extensive political and administrative reforms which were designed to allow more self-government in local island affairs. On September 28, 1958, the inhabitants of French Polynesia, in accordance with the Constitution of the Fifth Republic, voted to maintain the status as an Overseas Territory of the Republic.

The economy of the island has been basically agricultural, as the soil is very rich and requires little cultivation to make it produce a great variety of vegetables and fruits. Some of the products are mangos, bananas, papayas, breadfruit, oranges, and coconuts with their by-product copra, which is consistently less in demand by industry. Efforts are being made to develop the raising of livestock as well as to increase the production of mother of pearl.

Education is compulsory between the ages of six and fourteen and is free in public schools. (The large Chinese population on the island maintains its own school but has compulsory education in the French language.)

All is not sweetness and light on this island, of course. There are undercurrents here as in nearly every other country. The Tahitians are a proud and independent people; for example, when the French announced in 1958 that taxes would be imposed upon everyone, the Tahitians stormed the government buildings and created such a riot that the tax plan was abandoned. Occasionally there is talk of seeking independence from the French, and certainly there is a small faction of rebellious people; in 1959 Pouvanaa, considered one of the leaders of the Tahitian people, was jailed for many months on vague charges of insurrection against the authorities.

However, want and need and oppression are the basis for any successful political upheaval and the Tahitian people have too pleasant a life to worry much about politics; unless the recent and future influx of tourists manages to infect them with the worst of all the white man's many diseases—discontent—the modern history of Tahiti will remain placid and enviable for some time to come.

But the end of the road for the Tahitians and their way of life is tragically in sight; as Charles Warren Stoddard wrote so beautifully in *South Sea Idyls*:

Walking alone in those splendid nights I used to hear a dry, ominous coughing in the huts of the natives. I felt as though I were treading upon the brinks of half-dug graves, and I longed to bring a respite to the doomed race.

One windy afternoon we cut our stern hawser in a fair wind and sailed out of the harbor; I felt a sense of relief, and moralized for five minutes without stopping. Then I turned away from all listeners and saw those glorious green peaks growing dim in the distance; the clouds embraced them in their profound secrecy; like a lovely mirage Tahiti floated upon the bosom of the sea. Between sea and sky were swallowed up vale, garden, and waterfall; point after point crowded with palms; peak above peak in that eternal crown of beauty; and with them the nation of warriors and lovers falling like the leaf, but, unlike it, with no followers in the new season.

PART 3

Well—enough of history.

What is modern Tahiti like and what will you see when you get there?

Let's assume that you arrive by water. Perhaps you will be on a Matson liner from San Francisco or Los Angeles or a freighter from Panama. Again, it might be a private yacht, since Papeete is the goal of every sailor with any boat larger than thirty feet. Or it may be a chartered sailing vessel such as that of Captain Omer Darr, who is pictured in this chapter with his beautiful Hawaiian wife. (At this writing he has regular sailings every few months out of Sausalito, California, on his one-hundred-foot schooner.) You will sail in through the reef into what must be the most colorful harbor in the world. (The tiny island in the harbor, incidentally, which looks like the tropical island in cartoons on which shipwrecked people find themselves, is the quarantine station.)

After going through customs, a comparatively relaxed and easy process, you'll have to drive through the little town of Papeete to get onto the road to your hotel. I'm not sure any words can prepare you for your first look at this bustling little capital of Polynesia. Most people are disappointed that it is so modern and large. Of course it does have a lovely cathedral that is straight from Somerset Maugham, but it also has too many cars, too many people, and too many colorless buildings. The main shopping center, and the closest thing to a supermarket to be found on Tahiti, is the shop of Sin Tung Hing, known to everyone as Ah You's, after the owner's nickname. Here you can buy everything from frozen American steaks to the latest catch of bonito. They even have Coca-Cola, which is not widely accepted here as yet. The other little Chinese market patronized most frequently by foreign residents is Arupa's.

The main market place is a block away from Ah You's and is especially colorful early in the morning. On the way to it you will probably pass Mr. Émile Gauguin making his live-bait traps.

The most interesting street on Tahiti is the Bir Hakeim, named after an important battle the French won in Africa in World War II. This street, which runs along the quay, is where most of Papeete's business and social life takes place. Also, there is constant excitement engendered by the arrival and departure of boats.

You may see Sterling Hayden entertaining visitors aboard his schooner. Hayden, one of the finest deep-water sailors in the world, has sailed into this harbor many times over the last twenty-five years.

As you drive out of Papeete counterclockwise (from a bird's eye view) you will pass the post office. You will find that you spend a lot

WERNER STOY

The Te Vega, skippered by Captain Omer Darr, is shown here making the exciting run from Hawaii to Tahiti. The Te Vega is now located in Caribbean waters and Darr makes regular sailings from San Francisco to Tahiti on the Wanderer, Sterling Hayden's old schooner.

At left are Captain Darr and his wife, who, though she looks the way Tahitian girls should look, is from Hawaii.

135

Actor-author Sterling Hayden receives visitors aboard his yacht in Papeete harbor.

Spencer Weaver, hotelman and restaurateur, who commutes from Honolulu to his Hotel Tahiti, is married to a lovely Tahitian.

136

Paul Gauguin's son, Émile, perhaps the most familiar character on the Papeete scene. Occupation: fish-trap maker and autograph-signer.

of time in this building, since it often takes an hour in line to get one's mail. The building is indicative of the sad changes that are coming to Tahiti. The present building lacks all the charm of the lovely one torn down in 1959.

As long as we've started, let's go completely around the island, which, as you can see by the map, is somewhat like a frying pan with Tahiti-iti (or Little Tahiti) as the handle. The road, the one road, goes only around the main island. About one kilometer from the main part of town is the Hotel Tahiti, which is probably the nicest on the island. (The Grand Hotel in Papeete proper doesn't seem to have any Tahitian feeling about it.) The Hotel Tahiti was built by Spencer Weaver, a hotel and restaurant man from Honolulu, who is married to a Tahitian. The rates here are high, approximately twenty dollars a day for a bungalow for two, American plan, but the food and service are excellent.

Farther on down the road you come to Les Tropiques which is a similar bungalow-hotel operation and has been around for a much longer time. The owners claim that at least one tourist per Matson cruise comes in and asks for "Les."

The Faaa airport is the next landmark on our trip. Until 1960 one had to take a flying boat from Bora Bora, 141 miles to the northeast, but now, with the filling in of the lagoon and the creation of a landing strip, Tahiti has moved, for better or for worse, into the jet age. This three-million-dollar project started in May 1959, required a round-the-clock procession of fifty trucks to move enough valley stones to fill the little bay, and was finished in May 1961. At present two airlines, Air France and South Pacific Airlines, service Tahiti. The airport is five and a half kilometers from the center of town. (There are no addresses here; everything is known by the distance from Papeete.)

Eight kilometers from town one finds a charming old house which seems to me to symbolize the past glory of Tahiti in its crumbling present. It belonged to the Goupil family, but is now uninhabited, and cows wander around the elaborate statuary and movie companies film scenes against it.

137

MACKENZIE

The attractive old Post Office (ABOVE) *was torn down in 1959 to make way for the modern structure shown at right.*

CONRAD

138

I snapped a mound of coconut husks across the road from the Goupil house, which is just one of the many places where copra is dried. Copra is still one of Tahiti's main exports, but the coconut trees from which it is derived are dwindling in number. (The first question that every tourist asks is why there are metal bands on the trees and the answer is that they keep the rats from scaling them to get at the nuts.)

Near the thirteenth kilometer (the distances are marked on stones on the left-hand side of the road) you come to the place where Paul Gauguin lived from 1896 to 1901. He died on Nuka Hiva in 1903. It seems that whenever one goes to Tahiti friends always suggest that you "look around and pick up some cheap Gauguins." Even Rupert Brooke wrote a friend that one of the reasons he went to Tahiti was in the hope of discovering some of the master's works. The sad part of the story is that there were a great many Gauguins around after the artist's death, and it seems that every long-time resident of the island has a story about his family's burning some "worthless" Gauguin sketches. If you want to see a fascinating and depressing document, go to the little museum in Papeete, which is run by the highly capable Aurora Natua, and ask to see the list of paintings that were sold at auction in Papeete after Gauguin's death. Several now famous canvases went for the equivalent of a few dollars, but most were not sold at all and were subsequently burned. It was here that Gauguin lived with his Tahitian wife, who bore his son Émile.

Nearby you will see the quaintly named "Deux Plus Deux Egale Quatre Ecole." The person who donated the money stipulated that it must always be called the "Two Plus Two Equals Four School."

We are now in the district of Punaauia. There are fourteen districts on the main island and eight on the peninsula. In Punaauia and in the next district, Paea, you will see some of the handsomest homes on the island. My house for two summers was at 18.500 kilometers. This house and the one next to it, always referred to as the Countess's, are probably the nicest houses for rent on Tahiti.

"*Tahitian Landscape*" by Paul Gauguin (1848–1903). (*Courtesy Frick Collection.*)

"*Self Portrait*" *by Paul Gauguin.*

OPPOSITE: "*Two Tahitian Women*" *by Paul Gauguin. (Courtesy the Metropolitan Museum of Art.*)

140

The metal bands on the coconut trees keep the rats from scaling them to get at the fruit.

Les Tropiques, one of the oldest and most popular hotels on the island.

David Huntington, author of the delightful book *Tahitian Holiday*, lived in this latter house for six months in 1960, and he and I are responsible for creating the great sin against Tahiti—designing the first golf course on the island. We, however, refer to it as "flog," which is "golf" backward, due to its lack of similarity to the Scottish national sport. Land crabs, falling coconuts, myna birds, and chickens were only a few of the hazards on this five-hole ordeal.

At the nineteenth-kilometer mark on Sunday mornings you can find cock fights in progress and a group of enthusiastic rooters. Great sums of money are wagered at many of these pits all around the island and in Papeete itself. The birds themselves, if champion material, are often worth as much as a hundred dollars, and paradoxically the best fighters come from the Pacific coast of America.

Just beyond this cock-fight pit is one of the best canoe makers on the island, Teaitua. For the equivalent of fifteen dollars he made a splendid *vaa* for my son. Canoes are made by shaping the silk cotton trees with crude implements. The outriggers are subsequently made from the *purau* tree; the rear springy supports for the outrigger are made of guava and the front solid supports of rosewood. The making of *vaas* is an ancient and important art, since every family has at least one which they now use for fishing and in old Tahiti used for battle as well. The larger canoes are featured every year in the paddling contest which is a very important feature of the annual Bastille Day celebration.

At kilometer 23 you will see a sign on the left of the road saying "Marae of Arahurahu." This marae has been reconstructed and is in fine condition. Long-time residents believe firmly that to remove a rock from a marae will bring the worst possible luck, and all have horrendous stories as conclusive proof.

And then one comes to the Grottes de Maraa. These are the largest natural caves on the island.

Actually there are very few *specific* points of interest on the trip but the incredible views that one sees constantly, and the Tahitian types

A local boat builder, Teaitua, hollows out the trunk of a silk cotton tree to make an outrigger, or vaa, as it's called.

144

themselves, are what make the trip unforgettable. Also, there are lovely streams every mile or two where you can cool off *au naturel,* such as the one at the thirty-ninth kilometer, where Sterling Hayden and his children bathe. Nearby is the marae of Mahiatea, which was originally four times as large as the one at Arahurahu—and one of the largest in all Polynesia. In the 1890s a Scotch landowner dismantled part of it for its big rocks, and later the French government built a bridge with a good part of it. What remains, however, is still very impressive.

All along the road you will see families gathering. The Tahitians are extremely sociable, and where is there a better place for them to see their friends and watch life go by? When they greet you with *"Iorana, maitai oe"* (Greetings, are you well?) your reply should be *"E, maitai roa"* (Yes, very well).

Frequently total strangers will ask you to join them if they happen to be eating. In case you're not so lucky as to be invited to a big roast-pig feast, you'd better plan on eating lunch at the Chinese restaurant near Taravao, since it is one of the two restaurants you'll encounter on the rest of the trip around the island. If you turn right at Taravao you can go out to Tautira, where you'll see natives living more primitively than in Tahiti proper. Robert Louis Stevenson lived near here for a while, claiming he arrived just in time, before the island would be ruined; however, this area has changed very little since Stevenson's day.

Because the road doesn't continue, one must hire canoes to see the rest of Tahiti-iti. It's a beautiful trip by power *pirogue,* and the giant waterfall seen from the boat is spectacular.

Back on Tahiti proper we find that the windward side of the island presents a more rugged aspect than the leeward side. There are fewer fancy homes of the popaas here. But after Point Venus and on into Papeete the area becomes more populated again. Point Venus must still be as beautiful as when the first explorers found it and when Bligh

OPPOSITE: *This horse fording a stream becomes a modern Gauguin picture when photographed by Eliot Elisofon. (Courtesy Life.)*

MACKENZIE

Waterfalls and pools like these are, unfortunately, not as common as the old Dorothy Lamour movies would have you believe. But they do exist, though you generally have to walk far up into the valleys to find them. There are beautiful ones around Tautira.

O: ELIOT ELISOFON, COURTESY LIFE

DAVID HUNTINGTON

The cemetery for the rapidly increasing Chinese colony.

The tomb of Pomare V is crowned with a Benedictine bottle, representing the King's favorite drink.

CONRAD

150

GEORGE HOLTON

Dancers at a dusk ceremony re-enact ancient rites by a Marae pyramid.

151

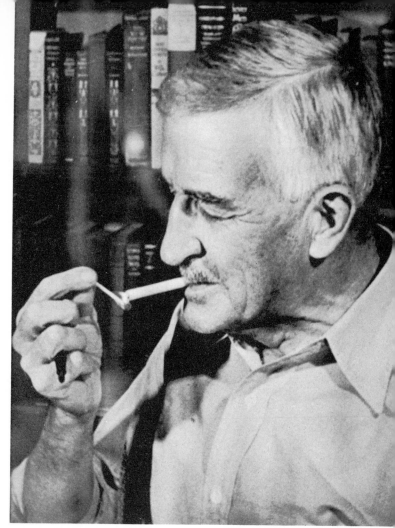

JAMES NORMAN HALL
APRIL 22, 1887 – JULY 6, 1951

LOOK TO THE NORTHWARD STRANGER,
JUST OVER THE HILLSIDE THERE,
HAVE YOU IN YOUR TRAVELS SEEN
A LAND MORE PASSING FAIR.

anchored in Matavai Bay back in 1788. A few large companies have threatened to put hotels nearby, but as yet they have been blessedly unsuccessful. The Lafayette night club, however (which doesn't open until midnight), is a noisy neighbor to the ghosts of the explorers.

The Chinese cemetery is worth stopping to see. Most of the markers contain photos or carved likenesses of the deceased.

In the hills above Matavai Bay lies buried one of the two men who probably did more to popularize the story of the *Bounty* than any other. James Norman Hall, who seems to have been the most popular man who ever lived on Tahiti, died in 1951, requesting that this inscription be put on his grave: "Look to the northward, stranger, Just over the hillside there, Have you in your travels seen A land more passing fair?" Hall's daughter Nancy, and her husband, Nicholas Rutgers, have built Tahiti's most modern home near Hall's grave overlooking this, the incredibly romantic Matavai Bay, the bay of Cook, the bay of the *Bounty*.

On the way into town you will pass the grave of King Pomare V. Like several of the other Pomare kings, this one was excessively fond of distilled spirits, and in a lovely ironic gesture his tomb is crowned by a gigantic Benedictine bottle, his favorite drink.

We next pass the Royal Tahitian Hotel and then the bleating of *les trucks* and the sputtering of the Solex power bikes and the hordes of handsome women on motor scooters tell us that we are once again in Papeete, and our tour of Tahiti is complete.

OPPOSITE: *James Norman Hall, co-author of* Mutiny on the Bounty *and one of the most popular men who ever lived in Tahiti. The photo at bottom is of the plaque marking his grave above the harbor of Matavai Bay, with the charming epitaph that he wrote for himself.*

Hints for the Traveler

To get to Tahiti an American must have an up-to-date passport, a tourist visa from a French Consulate in the United States, a vaccination certificate, and a round-trip ticket or the guarantee of return-passage costs made by a person living in French Polynesia.

At this writing the best air service is T.A.I., which has direct service from Los Angeles via DC-8 jet. The stewardesses are Polynesian girls; the food is excellent and the trip lasts only seven and a half hours. Round-trip economy fare is $754 and first class is $1022.

One's luggage is inspected by the customs with more or less diligence and adherence to the rules, depending upon the mood of the inspector. Four hundred cigarettes per person or fifty cigars or four hundred grams of tobacco are allowed.

Theoretically, one is allowed only one camera duty-free, but I have never seen that rule enforced. Only ten rolls of film and twelve dark slides per person are allowed. You are permitted one movie camera besides the still camera, but only ten rolls of film between the two of them. The duty is approximately fifty per cent on any extra films. It is smart to make your ten duty-free rolls of film Kodachrome, if you have a movie camera, because 16-mm. Kodachrome costs about fifteen dollars a roll in Papeete. There is plenty of film for still cameras at almost the same prices as in the United States.

You can have black-and-white film processed easily in Papeete, and even Ektachrome, but as yet there is no Kodachrome developing. Sometimes the processing is as good as it is at home, but sometimes it is not, so, if you can make yourself wait, it is smarter to take the films back to the United States with you.

The best photographic stores are: McKenzie's (he also has a good selection of his own work) on the Avenue Prince Hinoi; Sylvain's, next to the Vaima Café; and Sounam Photo, in an unprepossessing little shop on Maréchal Foch Street. You can rush to any of these shops the day before you leave and buy color slides of the dozens of shots you never quite got around to taking.

Most photographers are amazed by the extraordinary light in Tahiti. It is much brighter than you might think. It is smart to keep your exposed films in a large tin with some silica gel, as the tropic humidity can do terrible things especially to color film. Donald's store on the waterfront carries silica gel.

Although photographing of the official Bastille Day celebration dancing is not permitted, a special morning is set aside for camera addicts. No cameras are allowed, however, at the demonstration of fire walking. My wife didn't know this rule, took a flash photo of the walkers, and almost caused one to stumble and fall on the hot coals (which is the reason for the rule).

Guns can be brought in only with special authorization; there seems to be very little to shoot with one, anyway.

What to wear in Tahiti is relatively simple. It is strictly informal for both men and women at all times, and most European island residents wear a tie only on Bastille Day. The rest of the time men wear short-sleeved sport shirts and shorts or slacks, and sometimes it is cool enough in the evening to wear sweaters or a light-weight jacket. Women wear light cotton dresses night and day, and often a pareu-like dress that can be purchased in Tahiti. Sandals, moccasins, or tennis shoes are the usual footwear.

You can find just about any type of clothing you need in Papeete. The bathing suits and sports shirts made there are especially attractive in brilliantly colored floral prints and simple designs, and they make good presents. Marie Ah You has a good selection of all types of dresses, and is considered the Dior of Tahiti, rivaled only by Augustine. For men's shirts Tahiti Arts is perhaps the best store. And the Chic at 24 Rue de Général de Gaulle has the best selection of perfume (the best French products) at less than half the American price. For tiki statuettes, drums, baskets, hats, mats, shells, and so on, the best place is Cambridge Shiu's Société Manuia shop at 19 Rue de Général de Gaulle, where you can get anything from stuffed puffer fishes to an outrigger canoe, which Mr. Shiu will pack and send for you; he is a charming person and speaks perfect English.

If you are going to be in Tahiti for some time and want to hear something other than Tahitian music, a good idea is to bring a portable transistor phonograph, since electricity is hard to come by in Tahiti. There is a good selection of European, American, and Tahitian records to be found in Papeete, but they are expensive.

Should you bring children to Tahiti? I can't think of a better place for them. The milk is pasteurized, the water is good, and the food is wholesome. There are several good French doctors and a fairly modern hospital and two up-to-date pharmacies. Tahiti is a healthy place to live for both children and adults. There is no typhoid, malaria, yellow fever, or cholera; filariasis, which can lead to elephantiasis, is no threat to the

NEXT PAGE: *Dancing at Les Tropiques*
FRED LYON

tourist, since it takes long living on the island to become susceptible to it. Even if one has become exposed to it by the bite of a very rare mosquito, staying in a temperate zone kills the disease.

Swimming and shell collecting keep the children happy, to say nothing of coconut-tree climbing and other activities peculiar to Tahiti. Ours quickly made friends with the Tahitian children, and, though neither could speak the others' language at first, the lack of verbal communication seemed to bother no one.

The climate in Tahiti can be superb; the humidity is quite high, however, averaging about seventy-eight per cent. The dry season is supposedly from March to November, when temperatures vary between 62 to 76 degrees. In the wet season from December to February, the temperature generally stays between 72 and 88 degrees. January is the hottest month. Be warned that, although weather can be splendid, it can also rain for days and even weeks on end in either the wet or dry season.

For help about anything from shopping to acquiring a house, call on the Tourist Bureau on the waterfront; you can write to it at P.O. Box 65, Papeete, Tahiti, French Polynesia. Some of the very few luxurious houses are rented by John and Purea Reasin at five hundred dollars or more per month.

The best travel agencies in Papeete for round-the-island tours or trips to the outer islands are: Agence Tahiti Poroi, 101 Quai Bir-Hakeim, Papeete, P.O. Box 83; Tahiti Voyages, 3 Place Notre Dame, Papeete (across from the Cathedral); Ia Orana Tours, in the Bank Building near the Cathedral.

Cars are easy to rent in Tahiti from the Hertz representative, Dave Cave, or from the Avis people, with rates for small French cars comparable to those in the United States. Dave is a long-time Tahitian–resident American, and you will find him pleasant to deal with. You can also rent Vespa scooters and bicycles at various places on the island.

An exciting tour which many people miss is the visit to Tautira and from there by outrigger to the little island of Fenua Ino (Forbidden

Land). Here you will see a Tahiti that must look almost exactly the same as when Bougainville visited it.

The most beautiful waterfall on the island is the one called "Fachoda." To reach it takes about three hours by jeep and forty-five minutes by foot over mountain paths, but it is worth it.

Attendance at an authentic Tahitian feast can be arranged through any travel agent. In the exotic garden of Hapuatara tourists can watch the preparation of roast pork, Tahitian poe, coconut milk, and marinated raw fish. Afterward there is dancing and swimming or fishing.

Many tourists who come to the island never quite manage to get over to Mooréa. This is a mistake, for it is undoubtedly one of the most beautiful places in the world. As Austin Peterson has written:

To enter Cook's Bay, is like sailing into a cathedral. The sound of the diesel seems sacrilegious. All around you are the towering mountain peaks shooting crazily into the sky, shapes so weird you feel you are watching an earth being born. You almost expect a dinosaur to peek out at you from behind a crag.

Incidentally, that same Mr. Peterson has an unpretentious but complete guide to Tahiti in which he lists all the hotels, their addresses and prices, and the names and addresses of doctors, lawyers, and businessmen in Tahiti and Mooréa. It would be especially helpful for anyone thinking of investing in land or business on the island. Unbound and mimeographed, it is constantly being revised in the light of Tahiti's fast-changing scene and is available for two dollars from Mr. Peterson at 1872 Navajo Drive, Palm Springs, California.

People frequently want to go to other islands besides Tahiti and Mooréa. Perhaps the most beautiful is Bora Bora, 150 miles from Tahiti and accessible by air from there for approximately thirty-five dollars. The tiny main village of Bora Bora called Vaitape seems very primitive when compared to Tahiti. The one hotel that comes up to what Americans demand is a twenty-bungalow type called the Bora Bora

Hotel built by a San Franciscan, Bob Fraser; double accommodations cost about forty dollars per day, American plan. A much more primitive and correspondingly cheaper hotel is the Tiare Tahiti Hotel, with rates starting around two dollars a day.

As Stevenson said (of another island), Bora Bora touches a virginity of sense. Many people think that it is even more beautiful than Mooréa, and anyone who truly wants to get away from the comparative hustle and bustle of Tahiti should consider this island. There is not much to do in Bora Bora that you don't think up yourself. Hiking, fishing, and bicycling are about all there is, but the scenery is dazzling and the people are handsome and friendly.

Other islands close to Tahiti are Huahine, which is the nearest leeward island from Tahiti, and Raiatea, Aitutaki, and Rapa, all of which have uncertain transportation services. Tourist agencies can give you the schooner schedules.

For those who want to get away from civilization completely, there are the Marquesas, which lie about a week away from Tahiti by schooner. A round trip takes almost a month, since many stops are made, including those made at the Tuamotus. First class costs approximately five dollars per day with meals. It is a rough trip, but for the hearty and adventurous a rewarding one, since on it you will see bays, lagoons, atolls, and people that the traveler rarely sees.

There is talk of air service to the outer isles, but as yet that has not come to pass. However, it is inevitable, since the tourist trade is fast becoming Tahiti's main business. In 1955 there were less than 1000 tourists; by 1960 there were 5000, and it is estimated that by 1965 there will be 50,000. It seems now that Tahiti has a long way to go to catch up to Waikiki, but one wonders if it will seem such a great distance by, say, about 1975.

It is a saddening thought to the many people who have loved this unique place, this story-book island, this Great Tahiti of the Golden Haze.

Bibliography

ADAMS, HENRY. *Memoirs of Arii Taimai e Marama of Eimeo.* . . . Paris: privately printed, 1901.

AUBERT DE LA RUE, EDGAR. *Tahiti et ses archipels; Polynésie française.* Paris: Horizons de France, 1958.

CHEGARAY, JACQUES. *Tahiti l'enchanteresse.* Paris: Editions Sun, 1956.

CHRISTIAN, FREDERICK W. *Eastern Pacific Lands: Tahiti and the Marquesas.* London: R. Scott, 1910.

CLUNE, FRANK. *A Tale of Tahiti.* Sydney: Angus and Robertson, 1958.

DANIELSSON, BENGT. *Love in the South Seas.* New York: Reynal, 1956.

DAY, DOROTHY. *Tahiti; A Chapter in Pacific Imperialism.* Berkeley, California, 1933 (thesis).

FRISBIE, ROBERT DEAN. *My Tahiti.* Boston: Little, Brown, 1937.

FURNAS, J. C. *Anatomy of Paradise.* New York: Sloane, 1948.

GAUGUIN, PAUL. *Ancien culte mahorie.* Paris: La Paline, 1951.

———. *Noa-Noa.* Boston: Little, Brown, 1920.

GIBBRINGS, ROBERT. *Iorana! A Tahitian Journal.* Boston: Houghton Mifflin, 1932.

HALL, JAMES NORMAN. *Mid Pacific.* Boston: Houghton Mifflin, 1928.

HAWEIS, HUGH REGINALD. *Travel and Talk.* London: Chatto and Windus; New York: Dodd, Mead, 1896.

HENRY, TEUIRA. *Ancient Tahiti.* Honolulu: Bernice P. Bishop Museum, 1928.

HOLMSEN, SVERRE. *Polynesian Trade Wind.* (Translated from Swedish). London: J. Barrie, 1959.

HUNTINGTON, DAVID. *Tahitian Holiday.* New York: Henry Holt, 1954.

KEABLE, ROBERT. *Tahiti: Isle of Dreams.* London: Hutchinson, 1925.

KEELER, CHARLES AUGUSTUS. *Tahiti the Golden.* San Francisco Steamship Co., 1902.

LA FARGE, JOHN. *Reminiscences of the South Seas.* New York: Doubleday, Page, 1912.

LEMIRE, MARIE CHARLES DESIRE. *L'océanie française, les intérêts français dans la Pacifique.* Paris: Berger-Levrault, 1904.

LOUSSIN, JEAN MARIE. *Tahiti.* Paris: Edition de Seuil, 1957.

MICHENER, JAMES. *Return to Paradise.* New York: Random House, 1951.

MOERENHOUT, J. A. *Voyage aux îles du Grand Océan,* tome I and II. Arthur Bertrand, Librarie-Editeur, 1837.

MORRISON, J. *The Journal of J. Morrison.* London: Golden Cockerel Press, 1935.

PRIIE, WILLARD. *Adventures in Paradise; Tahiti and Beyond.* New York: Doubleday, 1955.

REY, LESCURE. *Abrège d'histoire de la Polynésie française, Tahiti et les archipels.* 1958.

ROBERTSON, GEORGE. (Master of H.M.S. *Dolphin*). *The Discovery of Tahiti; A Journal of the Second Voyage. . . .* London: Hakluyt Society, 1948.

ROWE, NEWTON ALLAN. *Voyage to the Amorous Island; the Discovery of Tahiti.* London: A. Deutsch, 1955.

STODDARD, CHARLES WARREN. *South Sea Idyls.* Boston: J. R. Osgood, 1873.

STROVEN, CARL, AND DAY, A. GROVE, EDS. *The Spell of the Pacific.* New York: Macmillan, 1949.

T'SERSTEVENS, ALBERT. *Tahiti et sa couronne.* Paris: A. Michel, 1950–1951.

VERNIER, ANDRÉ. *Echos et reflets de Tahiti.* Valence: Imprimeries Reunies, 1952.

VERNIER, CHARLES. *Tahitiens d'hier et d'aujourd'hui.* Paris: Société des Mission Évangeliques, 1948.

VILLARET, BERNARD. *Tahiti, le dernier paradis terrestre.* Paris: Amiot-Dumont, 1951.

VINCENDON-DEMOULIN, CLEMENT ADRIEN. *Iles Taiti.* Paris: A. Bertrand, 1844.